Life in a drop of water, magnified 100 diameters, showing minute animals and plants.

*A beginner's guide to exploring the
micro-world of plants and animals.*

HUNTING WITH THE

MICROSCOPE

GAYLORD JOHNSON

with additions by
MAURICE BLEIFELD
*Chairman, Biology Department
Newton High School, Elmhurst, New York*

*Illustrated with photo-micrographs
and explanatory line illustrations.*

SENTINEL BOOKS PUBLISHERS, INC.
New York 3, New York

Published by
Sentinel Books Publishers Inc.
17-21 East 22 Street, New York, N. Y. 10010

Revised edition
Copyright © August 1963 by
Sentinel Books Publ. Inc.

Additions by:
Charles Tanzer and Maurice Bleifeld.
ISBN 0-911360-23-9.

Cover photo courtesy of
Gilbert Division, Gabriel Industries, Inc.

Printed in the United States of America

CONTENTS

I

HOW TO USE THE "POCKET LENS"—
SIMPLEST MICROSCOPE OF ALL

Right at the beginning I want to exercise the author's privilege of giving unasked advice.

It's a warning. Here it is:

If you think you "can't afford a microscope," don't start playing with a pocket lens!

Before you know it, you'll catch "microscopitis," and there is no cure, except the possession of a really good compound microscope.

If you are ready to take the risk, I'll proceed to show you a few of the fascinating ways in which you can use even the cheapest, most ordinary magnifying glass to hunt wonders in the sub-size world.

The enticing thing about microscope hunting is that its achievements are progressive—and so are its thrills. You can begin with a pocket "linen tester" lens, and have a whale of a good time with it until you can acquire, perhaps, a "fountain pen" pocket microscope, giving you an enlargement of 30 or 40 times. Your next jump after that will be to an instrument magnifying 100 to 200 diameters.

TYPES OF LENSES FOR VARIED USES

This first chapter, however, is devoted entirely to a survey of pocket lenses and their possibilities. To begin with, what are the various kinds of "pocket" or "hand" lenses, and their merits,

The page of sketches (see Figure 1) shows a few of the forms in which you can get the simple microscope, or pocket lens, and the following paragraphs may help you in selecting the best one with which to start enjoying the pleasures of exploring the universe of the tiny.

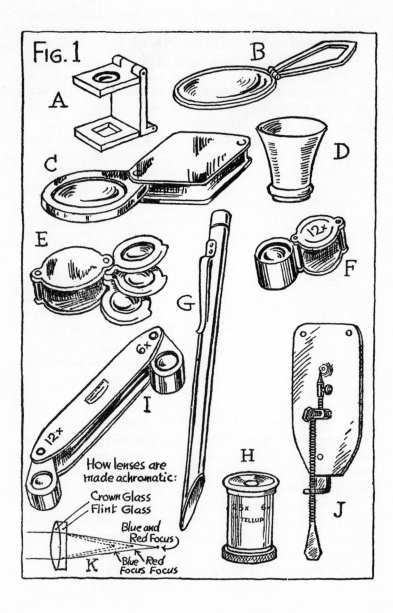

FIG. 1

How lenses are made achromatic:

Crown Glass
Flint Glass

Blue and Red Focus

Blue Red
Focus Focus

(A) *The Linen Tester*. As its name indicates, this glass is intended to count the number of threads per inch in linen and other fabrics. The bottom of the frame has a ¼ inch square opening, and the top carries a small double-convex lens which gives a magnification of about 3 diameters. Costs about $1.50. Larger sizes, more.

We have mentioned the word "diameters" two or three times, so it will be a good plan to stop right here and make its meaning plain. If you look at the 1/16-inch divisions on a rule with a glass which magnifies four diameters, the length of one of the divisions (seen through the glass) will apparently be equal to the length of four of them (seen with the naked eye). "Four diameters magnification," or simply "4x," means that the object is shown through the glass four times as wide and four times as long as it appears without the glass.

In the advertising of cheap microscopes, you sometimes read that an instrument "magnifies over 1,000 times," or something equally amazing. The figure refers of course to the "surface area" of the magnified object, obtained by multiplying the width-enlargement by the length-enlargement. The actual magnification in diameters is therefore in this case only about 32.

(B) *Folding Pocket Lens*. A convenient type for carrying constantly in the pocket to inspect small objects in a general way. These folding lenses vary in power from 3 to 5 diameters. The main advantage is the large field. They are really only reading glasses in miniature. This type should be carried in a slip case to prevent scratching the glass, which ruins its efficiency. Costs about $1 and up.

(C) *Another Folding Type*. This is a better all-round type than (B) because it closes into a protective frame for carrying. Some of the best opticians put out their lower power pocket lenses in this model. Costs

$1.25 and up, depending upon quality and manufacturer.

(D) *Watchmakers' "Loupe," or Eye-Glass*. This is simply a three or four-power lens of short focus, mounted into a rubber tube for holding in the eye, like a monocle, in order to leave both hands free for watch-repair work. This lens is sometimes a convenience when examining flowers or insects. The object can be held in one hand, and its parts moved with a pin or tooth-pick in the other, while the eye-socket holds the magnifier. Costs $1.25 and up. Sometimes more when especially powerful and with double lens.

(E) *Multiple Folding Lens*. This type is provided with two or three lenses of different powers, all folding into the handle. The lenses are meant to be used singly or in combination. This looks at first sight like a convenient arrangement, but will be found clumsy and irritating in use. It always needs to have lenses folded in or out. It is much better to carry a wide-field, lower-power lens of 3 or 4 diameters for getting a general look, and another smaller high-power lens of 10 or 12 diameters for details. Costs $4 or more.

(F) *Folding High Power Lens*. Most of the fine opticians (such as Zeiss, Leitz, Spencer and Bausch and Lomb) put out their higher power magnifiers in some form similar to this. This type of magnifier varies from 5x to 20x, and sometimes even 30x. Lenses of these powers must of course be corrected for color; they must be "achromatic" (literally, "without color"). Costs $6 and more, depending upon power and maker.

Let us take a short detour and see what "achromatism" means to your seeing ability. If you take a simple "single" lens (made from only one piece of glass; a reading lens, let us say) and strain it to the limit of its magnifying power, you will see a fringe of orange and blue color around the object at which you are looking.

This indicates that the spectrum-colored rays making up the light are bent unequally by their passage through the lens, just as they are through a prism. This effect is not a serious detriment to the efficiency of a 3- or 4-diameter magnifier, but it is to a 10 or 12 power lens, because the rays are bent so much more in causing the higher magnification that the color fringes are much more troublesome. Accordingly, all higher power magnifiers are "double" or "achromatic" lenses. The diagram at (K) in *Figure 1* shows how the bending of the colored rays caused by a lens of one kind of glass is corrected by one made from another kind of glass—a kind which has a different light-bending power.

If you ask an optician for an "achromatic" pocket lens of this higher-powered type, he will perhaps say that they are all "aplanatic." This word is more frequently used in connection with magnifiers and means exactly the same as "achromatic." It may be well to mention here that the very finest pocket magnifiers of all are "anastigmatic," just as the finest camera lenses are "anastigmats."

You may think that the prices of good high-power pocket lenses are too high—and you may wonder that the smaller the lens, the higher the price as well as the power—but such a lens, once purchased, will never wear out, and will be a constant source of satisfaction in dozens of ways. The writer has a 12x "aplanat" which he always carries in his vest pocket for emergency use in seeing small objects of every description. Ten years ago it cost $5, and, aside from a few worn spots where the nickel is off, the glass is as good as new. It has given much more than 50 cents a year in pleasure.

(G) *Fountain Pen Type Magnifier.* This type of hand lens really falls into the class of the compound microscope, for it is not one lens but two. The lens nearer your eye magnifies the image formed by the lens nearer the object. However, this magnifier is included here, since it is carried and used as a pocket lens, being only about 25X in power. This type of instrument is excellent because it does not require the object to be held so close to the eye as is the case with a folding lens of corresponding magnification. Usually costs $2.50 and up; frequently seen advertised by mail order houses.

(H) *Combined Telescope and Magnifier.* Here is an ingenious little device which is only about an inch long and which can be used either as a 2½-power telescope or opera glass, or as a 6-power magnifier. It is made under different trade names, such as "Tellup" and "Telefier." The latter word, which is compounded of "telescope" and "magnifier" describes the abilities of the instrument. It is convenient both for examining small objects and looking at a distant view. Any optician can order one for you by either of the names given. Costs about $5 or $6. This type cannot, however, take the place of a good high-power pocket lens of the (F) type.

(I) *Double Pocket Lens Type.* This arrangement is the ideal one for the nature lover, for it provides two lenses of different powers folding into the convenient metal handle. With one lens of 5x or 6x and the other of 12x to 20x, the observer is equipped to examine any small object as thoroughly as is possible without the aid of a compound microscope. Costs $21 or more, depending upon the powers of the lenses and the maker.

(J) *The First Microscope.* This type of magnifier is illustrated here merely to show that the original "microscope" (invented by Leeuwenhoek of Holland in the late 17th Century was really nothing but a single pocket lens. Focusing was done with a screw which regulated the distance of the lens from the object. This tiny, much-curved lens was mounted between two thin silver plates. The object, placed on the point of a needle, was viewed through an opening scarcely larger than a pinhole. By thus restricting the opening of the lens, Leeuwenhoek was able to do away with the color fringes to a great extent. He constructed this type of microscope with lenses varying in power from 50 to 150 diameters, and with them made many of the pioneer discoveries in the microscopic science. Needless to say, he ground all his own lenses.

I might fill this part of the chapter entirely with the names and descriptions of objects in which your pocket lens will reveal new and unsuspected interests and beauties. There is really no end to the fascinating revelations you can enjoy with only a modest-powered glass of 10 or 12 diameters.

The stinging hairs on a nettle leaf—the mould on damp bread—the spiral drinking proboscis of a moth or butterfly—the leg of a bee, with its wonderful "baskets" for carrying pollen—the tongue of a bee—the wings of insects—the noise apparatus of a house-cricket—the eggs of many different sorts of insects—the stamens and pistils of flowers—these are only a few of the thousands of objects in which the owner of a good pocket lens can discern marvelous structures and mechanisms.

I might, as I say, describe some of them—but it would make dull reading—and I shall not do it. Instead, I am giving you as many simple sketches as I can of some of these objects which invite your scrutiny through the pocket lens—your "sharper eye." It will be much more fun for you than reading what they look like—and, still better, you'll know what you're looking for.

Here's an instance of what I mean: If I tell you that the honey bee has a "market basket" upon each

FIG. 2.

of her hind legs, you will probably think of a picture something like *Figure 2*. That is absurd of course. But if I draw you a fairly *true* picture of the way the bee's "basket" really looks, as in *Figure 3*, you will look at the next bee you see upon a flower with a thrill of real expectancy. You will then know what to look for; you will be curious to see the basket for yourself, and eager to point it out to others.

There is the "basket," stuffed full of the yellow pollen dust. How firmly the curving, springy hairs hold in the little yellow mass of sticky golden "flour" that is to make the "bread" of baby bees in the home hive! Even while you watch through a reading glass lens, the bee (oblivious of your scrutiny) is using her fore-legs to pack still more into the tiny receptacle. Do you wonder that this wonderful device is called a "basket?"

Scores of visual adventures like this await you and your two lenses—the wide-field one for examining scenes "in action," and the shorter-focused, more powerful one for examining the structures of the insect you have caught and killed. You can do this easily in a wide-mouthed bottle with a little household ammonia absorbed into a circle of blotting paper on the bottom. In a few minutes the insect is dead, and ready for detailed examination.

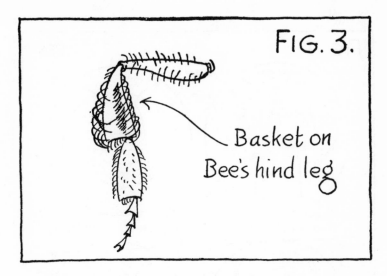

FIG. 3.

Basket on
Bee's hind leg

With your pocket lenses to aid your own sight, you can at once start out upon a journey into a country that is strange and new, but not far away. Step into the nearest garden, field or city park, and you are at once in the center of this unexplored territory—this land of little things. But nature finishes the tiniest insect with most exquisite care. In the jaws, legs and eyes of the first grasshopper or dragon fly you catch, your lens will reveal a beauty and ingenuity which will fascinate you with their wonder.

The best service I can do you now is to provide some pictures which indicate the features you should look for in the structures of insects—for these offer one of the most interesting of all fields for the pocket lens, just as the minute life of a pond offers the best objects for the compound microscope. We will investigate this later.

For the sake of the remarkable contrasts to be noted, we shall look at the same structure or organ as found in several different insects. For example, the pictures

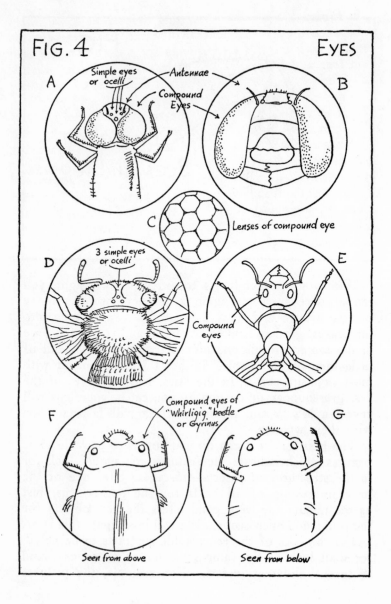

FIG. 4   EYES

A — Simple eyes or ocelli — Antennae — Compound Eyes

B

C — Lenses of compound eye

D — 3 simple eyes or ocelli

E — Compound eyes

F — Compound eyes of "Whirligig" beetle or Gyrinus — G

Seen from above   Seen from below

in *Figure 4* show the interesting differences to be noted between the *eyes* of several different creatures. In the same way, *Figure 5* represents the varieties to be seen in *legs* and *Figures 6* and *7* show the styles in *mouths*.

The pictures are the important things, but I am going to make a few running comments on them as we go along.

A in Figure 4. One of the most wonderful pairs of eyes in the whole world belongs to the dragon fly, and he has also a most wonderful set of wings. (These two facts go together, as you will see.) The dragon fly is almost never still. He will not stay to be examined. He must be caught in an insect net, and popped into the ammonia bottle until he is dead and quiet. Then you can look at his wonderful eyes through your lens.

Can it be that those two great dark rounding masses that meet on top of the head and extend forward and down on each side of the mouth are really eyes? They cover nearly the entire head, or at least two-thirds of it!

When the dragon fly poises motionless for a second in the air, like a humming bird, his great search-lights of eyes look north, south, east and west, above and below—all ways at once. He can see his prey in any direction, and his powerful wings take him instantly in pursuit.

Now look through your lens again at the top of the dragon fly's head. What do you see in that triangular space between the two great curving eyes? Two short, pointed horns or feelers—and three little round dots or knobs, close under the edge of the big eyes. The three little knobs are also eyes, but simple ones.

Now turn the creature so that his mouth faces you.

B in Figure 4. Observe the surface of the great eyes closely. It is dull, not shiny black. With a pocket lens magnifying only 5 diameters, you cannot see that the whole area of both eyes is covered with a myriad of little six-sided dots. But with a lens magnifying 20 times or more, you could see them quite plainly. They look like the ends of the cells in a honey bee's comb. What are they? Eyes, every one! Each of the tiny hexagons, which look, under a microscope, something like *C in Figure 4*, has a lens and an optic nerve and makes a clear picture of what is directly in front of it. We know this because miniature photographs have been taken with these lenses.

D in Figure 4. After looking so carefully at the head of the dragon fly, you quickly recognize all the same parts in the bee's head. You see the large compound eyes, the three little black knobs, or simple eyes, and the feelers or antennae.

They are the same in a general way, but very different in detail. The eyes are not great half-globes covering nearly all the head, but more moderate in size, and placed wide apart. They are strangely hairy too. The little simple eyes are more prominent and the feelers much larger.

Here again nature has supplied the creature with exactly the kind of tools needed for its life, for the bee makes great use of her feelers, and does not really need such all-seeing eyes as the fierce, meat-hunting dragon fly does.

E in Figure 4. Now let us take one of the large black ants which are crossing our path. We will interrupt her business long enough to have a look at her head. If you pick her up carefully, you can hold her quiet in your fingers without killing her in the ammonia bottle.

What a strange looking head! What large feelers! What prominent jaws! And the eyes, how comparatively small they are, sitting on each side of the black head. The ant's eyes are large enough, of course, to be very useful, but, since it walks every where as a rule instead of flying, it has many more opportunities to use a good pair of feelers. So they grow very large. The ant not only feels with them, but probably also smells with them, and most certainly talks to other ants with them. With all these uses for her antennae, it is no wonder that nature makes them grow large, many-jointed and pliable.

F in Figure 4. A few steps down our road the surface of a pond is rippling in the breeze. What are those shiny little black things circling round each other so rapidly near shore? "Whirligig Beetles," and well named. The scientific name is *Gyrinus,* which is related to "gyrate." Catch one in your pond-net. It looks like a small black bean of some kind. Pick it up gently between your thumb and finger and have a look at its head through your lens. Look at it first from above.

The whirligig's large eyes are wide apart, but still some distance from the margin of its head. They do not curve down over the sides, as in the bee and dragon fly.

Now turn the little beetle over and look carefully at its underside, the side that is in contact with the water when it is rushing in rapid circles. Remarkably enough, the whirligig seems to have another pair of eyes upon the under-side of its head, a pair of "water telescopes," so that no matter how the breeze stirs the surface, or how many ripples it makes itself, it can always see its prey in the water below with its under pair of eyes while the upper pair is watching out for danger from the air.

Actually, however, there is only *one* pair, which are divided inside the beetle's head, one part extending to the upper surface, and the other part to the lower surface.

A in Figure 5. And now to view the styles in legs. *Figure 5* shows for comparison a few of the legs of some common insects. Let us begin with the bee. After you have caught and killed one in an ammonia bottle, the front of her head, with its feelers and two fore legs, looks something like this picture. Even before you look

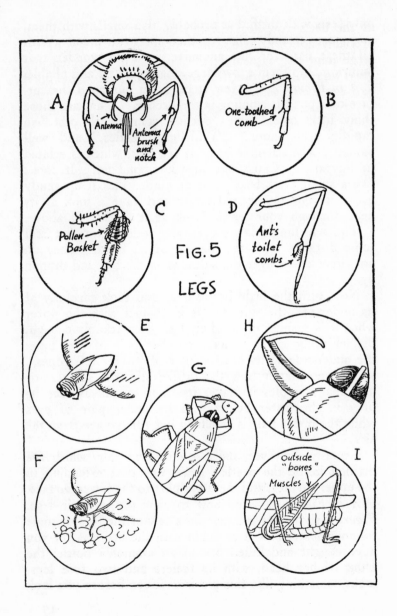

FIG. 5

LEGS

A — Antenna; Antenna brush and notch

B — One-toothed comb

C — Pollen Basket

D — Ant's toilet combs

I — Outside "bones"; Muscles

at the bee's fore leg through the lens at all, you will probably notice a little round notch on the inside of the large joint that is nearest the bee's foot. Through the glass you will see that it is quite a deep notch, a good half-circle, and that over it a little spike or pointed brush of stiff hairs projects down from the part of the leg above the joint.

Look at the round, smooth feeler on the bee's forehead—and then look back to the round notch on the foreleg, just within convenient reach of the feeler. The feeler and the notch are both round, and about the same size. The feeler would just fit into the notch, and, if drawn through it, the brush of hair would sweep off any dust that might be upon the feeler. So the notches and brushes on the lady bee's forelegs are really toilet utensils for her to use in keeping her antennae always spick and span.

B in Figure 5. If you look at the same joint of the bee's second leg, you can see, even without the lens, a sharp spike projecting downward, just as the "brush" does in the foreleg. Through your glass it looks like a long sharp thorn. This is also a toilet utensil, a kind of "one-toothed comb" to help the bee in keeping her legs always well-groomed.

C in Figure 5. Looking at the hind leg. You see how the limb is made broad and flat in order to provide a wide bottom for the basket; and how the sides, formed of stiff, springy hairs, curve up over the wide groove in the middle section of the leg. Next time you see a bee on a sunflower (which furnishes her with an abundance of pollen) notice how full these baskets can be stuffed without spilling their loads.

Now we shall need to pay another visit to the pond where we caught our "whirligig" when we were comparing the eyes of insects. We will take our dip net, and an ordinary tumbler in which to observe the working of a very remarkable pair of legs.

But on the way to the pond let us once more pick up a large ant, hold her under the lens and see if she has any leg-devices as clever and useful as the bee's.

D in Figure 5. Ants are just as neat as bees! The pocket-lens shows that the ant also has an "antenna cleaner," in the same joint of the foreleg where the bee carries hers. But it is not a groove and brush this time, but two little combs. The ant draws her feelers through these two combs just as the bee pulls hers through the groove-and-brush cleaner. Set the ant down on the road again and let us see what strange kinds of legs await us in the pond.

E in Figure 5. Stoop down and look sharply into the shallows near shore. Perhaps you will see a creature that has a very remarkable pair of legs indeed. Ah, he is really there! Do you see that little seed-shaped thing, less than half-an-inch long, advancing through the water by jerks? Indeed he *is rowing*—just like a man in a boat! No wonder he is called the "water-boatman." Scoop him up with the net and put him into the tumbler full of water with a few little pebbles in the bottom. Then perhaps you can see those wonderful little "oars" with one of your lenses.

Do you see those fringes of hair along the edges of his "oars?" As the oar comes forward, toward the head, the hairs are drawn forward limply, without making any resistance. But when the "water boatman" makes his "stroke," the hairs spread out, thrusting backward powerfully, and the boat leaps ahead.

F in Figure 5. Now the insect has come to rest for a moment. His long middle pair of legs are grasping one of the little pebbles in the bottom of the tumbler. The front pair are tucked up under the head. The "oars" are spread out on either side. This is how the water boatman looks when at rest.

Probably he was originally equipped with six legs, but, when his ancestors took to the water, two of them became adapted for swimming, the others being used for walking and standing.

Another pond insect has learned the same lesson of economy. This is the Giant Water Bug, called "Belostoma" by scientific men.

Sweep your net around over the pond bottom under those weeds near shore, and see whether you have luck. If you do, you won't be in doubt, for Belostoma deserves his name—he is sometimes over three inches long!

Up with the net—and there, in the midst of the dead leaves and trash, is a fair-sized Belostoma—and he is eating a baby sun-fish only an inch long!

G in Figure 5. You do not need a magnifying glass to see how he does it. He has seized the baby fish with his strong, tong-like claws. With them he is holding the prey close under his head, while he sucks the fish's blood through the sharp, strong beak that is plunged deep into its flesh. In handling the giant water bug you must have a care, for he can inflict a painful sting in your finger with that same beak.

I said a moment ago that Nature had made Belostoma learn the same lesson of economy that the water boatman had learned. You see at once that the giant bug has only four legs to walk with. The pair of tongs holding the baby fish is the other pair of legs—useless now for walking, but very useful to Belostoma for seizing his dinner as it swims past!

H in Figure 5. If you look through the lens at one of the tongs, you will see that the thick, heavy part has a groove, in the side next the head. Into this groove the smaller, sharp-pointed part of the tong folds. It

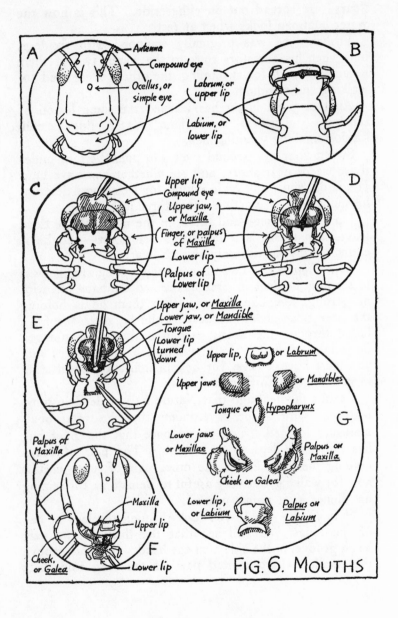

FIG. 6. MOUTHS

fits into the thick part as the blade of your pocket knife closes into its handle.

I in Figure 5. There goes a locust, wrongly called a "grasshopper" by some people. Watch where he lands, and sweep the insect net down over the spot. You have him. Take him out and look at his wonderful leaping legs with your pocket lens.

How thick and muscular the part nearest his body is! The pretty pattern on the side of the limb shows where the big leaping muscles are. Those little diamond-shaped spaces are their ends. Along the sides of this patterned surface run two strong, curved bands. They form a sort of oval picture-frame around the muscles; then they join together and make the joint for the straight, stiff part of the leg.

In *your* leg the muscles are attached to bones which run *inside,* through the center. They are deep out of sight. But in the locust's leg, the "bones" are *outside.* It is the same with the bee, the ant and other insects. They have no backbone, no inside skeleton. The supporting frame-work of an insect is always outside, in plain sight.

Are the different kind of mouths that insects eat with as interesting and wonderful as the varieties of eyes and legs? Yes, and you will be able to investigate them yourself—with your pocket lens. The pages of pictures in *Figures 6 and 7* will serve as your guide and show you what to look for with your lens.

Figure 6 will show how you can use a common locust or "grasshopper" to learn the principal parts of a typical insect's mouth. Then *Figure 7* will give you an exercise in identifying these various parts under a number of strange and remarkable "disguises."

Just a few running comments on these two pages of pictures, and then we must get into the next chapter and consider the "compound" microscope, which you may already be impatient to investigate.

A in Figure 6. The locust has the best mouth to start with. What a strange face! A little like the head of a "bock beer" goat. You notice at once the large compound eyes, the ocelli, and the antennae. Where are the mouth parts we are going to examine carefully with our pocket lens?

There, at the lower end of the locust's face, is something that looks like an upper lip. Insert the point of a pin under it and see if it moves. It is not of flexible, soft flesh, like your lips. Rather it is quite stiff and horny, but it can be moved up and down upon the hinge that joints it to the face.

B in Figure 6. Now let us find the other parts of the mouth. What about the locust's jaws? How are they different from ours? Let us see. Take the pin again. Lift up the upper lip and hold it. What is that shiny, dark brown mass that is revealed?

It must be the locust's upper jaw. See if you can find the teeth. They are not where you would expect to find them, are they? But the jagged line running across the brown mass from upper to lower lip looks like two rows of saw-teeth meeting. Try to insert the point of the pin into this line, and see what happens.

D in Figure 6. The pin makes the hard, dark mass divide; the two halves move apart sideways! It is plain that the locust's jaws are not like ours, opening and closing up and down. Instead, they open out to right and left. The teeth, too, you notice, are not set into the jaw, like those of animals, but are merely sharp points of the jaw itself.

E in Figure 6. Now, while you hold the jaws apart with your pin, watch through the lens while I take another pin and turn down the flap-like lower lip. This reveals another pair of jaws—the lower pair, called the "mandibles." These are smaller, with fewer teeth on their edges. When you have pushed your pin a little farther down, this lower pair will also open up sidewise. Instead of two jaws, like ours, the locust has four—an upper pair, called the "maxillae," and this lower pair, the mandibles.

Just below and between the lower jaws, you will see the locust's tongue, called the "hypo-pharynx," projecting from the cavity of the mouth. Now we have found all the parts of the mouth—two lips, four jaws and a tongue, except one, the cheeks.

F in Figure 6. Turn the locust so that we can look at his head a little from one side. Then lift up, with a pin point, that little flexible flap that covers the side of the lower jaw.

That is the locust's "cheek," or "galea." It is really attached to the lower jaw.

Now that we have seen all the different parts of the locust's mouth, we are ready to try to recognize the same mouth parts in some other insects. It will not be easy, for we shall find them masquerading under many disguises.

G in Figure 6. Perhaps, however, it will be a good plan to remove all the parts of the locust's mouth and glue them firmly to a little card. Then we can see at a glance how the parts of the bee's or butterfly's mouth differ from the locust's. These variations to meet special needs are shown in *Figure 7*.

A in Figure 7. Here is a full-front view of the honey bee's face, as seen through your pocket lens. Notice that the edges of the mandibles, or upper jaws, are not toothed. Nothing that the bee eats needs chewing. So the bee needs no teeth like the locust's. But the bee has learned to use these jaws as molding or modelling tools for shaping the wax of which her cells are built. Hence their smooth, spoon-like form.

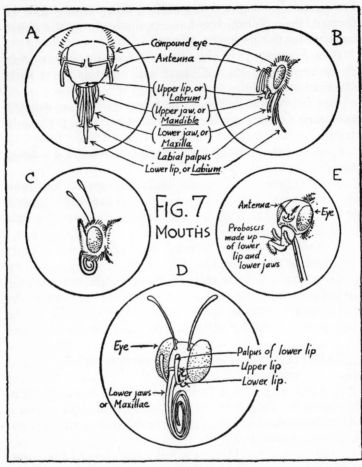

FIG. 7
MOUTHS

Labels in figure:
A, B
- Compound eye
- Antenna
- (Upper lip, or *Labrum*)
- (Upper jaw, or *Mandible*)
- (Lower jaw, or *Maxilla*)
- Labial palpus
- Lower lip, or *Labium*

C

E
- Antenna →
- ← Eye
- Proboscis made up of lower lip and lower jaws

D
- Eye →
- Palpus of lower lip
- Upper lip
- Lower lip.
- Lower jaws or Maxillae →

What can be the purpose of those five long parts that project down between the upper jaws? Scientists tell us that when the bee took to living upon the nectar of flowers, her lower jaws, or "maxillae," became greatly lengthened, and hollowed out on the undersides. The lower lip was also lengthened immensely, and so were its two labial "palpi." So now, when the bee holds these

26

five parts closely fitted together, a long strong tube is formed, through which the insect can suck up the sweet liquid from the hearts of flowers.

B in Figure 7. If you turn the bee so you can look at its head from the side, and separate the parts with a pin point, as shown here, your lens will show you more plainly how the eight mouth parts of the bee are related to the parts which correspond to them in the locust's mouth.

C in Figure 7. This is a butterfly's head, seen from the side.

Long antennae—immense compound eyes—and what else? What is that long, spirally-curved dark thread under the head? Pull it downward a little with a pin point, and it springs back, like the hair-spring of a watch. You guess quite rightly that it is a "sucking tube," something like the proboscis of the bee, but you would never guess what mouth-parts have been changed and modified to form it.

Take the pin again and unroll the little spring to its full length. See how long it is? It enables the butterfly to suck the nectar from deep, narrow flowers. Evidently the insect depends entirely upon its flexible soda-straw when it wants to eat.

D in Figure 7. It will be useless to guess at the identity of the parts that form it until we remove the coating of fuzzy hairs which cover the whole head and face. By scraping carefully with the point of a sharp pen knife, and then using a very small, dry water-color brush, the hairs rub off easily. When the whole head and face are thoroughly cleaned, it will look like this through your pocket lens.

Now we see that the sucking-tube is made from the maxillae, the two lower jaws. They have been enormously lengthened, grooved on the inner sides, and fitted together to make a "soda straw" for the butterfly.

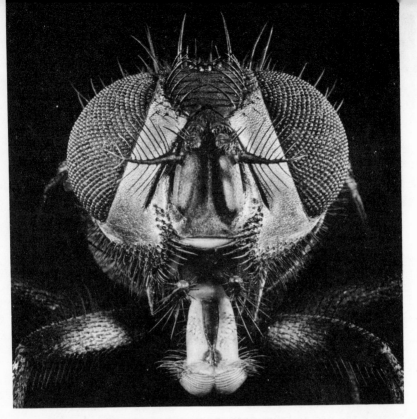

Fig. 8. Domestic House Fly, head-on view.
Courtesy of American Museum of Natural History

E in Figure 7. The common house fly is another insect which gets its food entirely by sucking up liquids. As a result of having no food that needs chewing, both its upper and lower jaws have practically disappeared. Take a look at its face through the lens, while you hold the proboscis, or sucking organ, extended downward with a pin. Notice that this kind of a sucking organ is devised to take liquids from flat, open surfaces, upon which the fly stands, while the butterfly's slender "hose-reel" is contrived so that it can reach down into the deepest, narrowest places in the blossoms of flowers, which flies never visit for food.

II

WHAT MAKES A COMPOUND MICROSCOPE REVEAL THE INVISIBLE

To begin, just what *is* a "microscope?"

To say that the word comes from two Greek ones— *mikros* (little)—and *skopein* (to look at), tells nothing that we didn't know already. Most people would naturally answer the question by saying that a microscope is an optical instrument for looking at very small objects, or an instrument which makes visible objects which are so tiny that man never even suspected their existence until the microscope was invented. These objects are so small that they are entirely below the range of the unaided human eye's seeing ability.

Another way of putting it is this: These microscopic objects are so "far away" in space from the human eye that they are "invisible": it cannot see them until they are brought *closer to it* by the microscope.

This new way of thinking about the magnifying power of a microscope may strike you as useless and uncalled for in a book of first steps in microscopic work, but be patient a moment and see if it doesn't help to make clearer everything else that I have to say about the magnifying powers of this remarkable instrument.

What do you do when, on a country walk, you catch sight of some interesting object off at one side of your path? Move nearer to it, of course, in order to see its details more clearly. Or, if it is a bird, which will fly away if you approach it, you make use of your field glass. If the glass is, let us say, of "six power" or six diameters, it means that you have actually placed your eye six times nearer to the bird.

If you doubt the literal truth of this statement, try the following experiment:

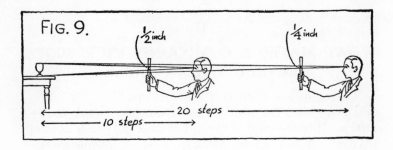

FIG. 9.

½ inch

¼ inch

20 steps

10 steps

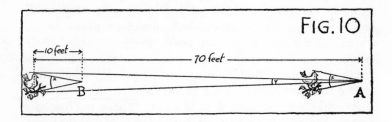

FIG. 10

10 feet

70 feet

B

A

Place a tumbler (or any other lumpish object) on a table. Stand twenty steps from it and measure its height on a ruler held at arms-length. (See *Figure 9.*) Let us say that the tumbler, at this distance, measures a quarter of an inch high on the ruler.

If you take ten steps toward the tumbler, you have placed your eye twice as near to the object. It should, accordingly, appear twice as large, or high, to your eye, and if you measure it on the arms-length ruler you will see that the glass tumbler now measures half an inch on the ruler. Each time you halve the distance between your eye and the object, you double the size it appears to your eye. (Note *Figure 9.*)

After you have walked *toward* the tumbler, and proved that its size on the ruler varies with your eye's distance from it, walk backward and measure your distance from the tumbler by noting the size it measures on the ruler.

The rule works both ways. If the tumbler is half an inch high at one standpoint and only a quarter of an inch high at another, you know that the second standpoint is twice as far away as the first.

Now think again of the bird (seen six times larger to your eye the moment you look through your field glass) and see if you aren't ready to admit that your eye is "actually" brought six times closer to the bird by the magnifying power of the field glass. If you doubt it, look at *Figure 10.*

In this diagram (A) is the standpoint from which you look at the bird 70 feet away. To your naked eye, it occupies the angle (Y), but when you look through your six-power glass, the bird occupies the angle (Z). Now see how much nearer to the bird you must be to have it occupy the angle (Z) to your naked eye. You must advance to the standpoint (B) only 10 feet away. At this point (B) you can see the bird as distinctly with the naked eye (provided you have normal vision) as you do through the glass at standpoint (A)—*because the bird occupies the same angle in both cases.*

You can see immediately what is meant when a telescope is spoken of as "bringing the moon to an apparent distance of fifty miles." It means that a one-mile wide crater on the moon (as seen through the instrument) apparently occupies the same visual angle as it would if seen by the naked eye at a distance of only fifty miles.

But when your naked, unassisted eye sees the moon, the individual crater (one mile across) is "invisible." In other words, *it occupies too small an angle at the human eye to be perceived.*

Now you know why microscopic objects were "invisible" to our eyes until the microscope was devised. They occupy too small angles at the human eye to be perceived.

What is the smallest angle which the human eye can perceive? It must be much smaller than a single "degree"

of arc, for the moon occupies the angle of ½ a degree.
(See *Figure 11*). A good way to find out is to see how
wide apart double stars in the sky must be, before the
eye can see them as separate. Few people can see the
space between a pair of tiny stars in the *Pleiades*. They
are about 3 "minutes," or 1/20 of a degree, apart.
Accordingly we can say that the average human eye can
begin to perceive details in objects only when they occupy
an angle of 2 or 3 minutes of arc.

You will perceive from this that the purposes of the
telescope and the microscope are identical: to increase
the angle which an object apparently occupies at the
human eye, and thus to bring the object apparently *closer*
to the eye. In fact, it may be said that the telescope
and the microscope *are* the same instrument, except that
each is modified to fulfil its purpose with a maximum of
efficiency.

An example (illustrated in *Figure 12*) shows how the
rays of light are bent in passing through a telescope
and a microscope—each of which magnifies one hundred
diameters.

The telescope is focussed upon the moon, which occupies an angle of ½ a degree in the human eye, when
240,000 miles away—and the microscope is focussed
upon a micro-organism which likewise occupies an angle
of ½ a degree at the naked eye, when 10 inches away.

In each case the angle which the object occupies at
the unaided eye is about ½ a degree of arc—and in

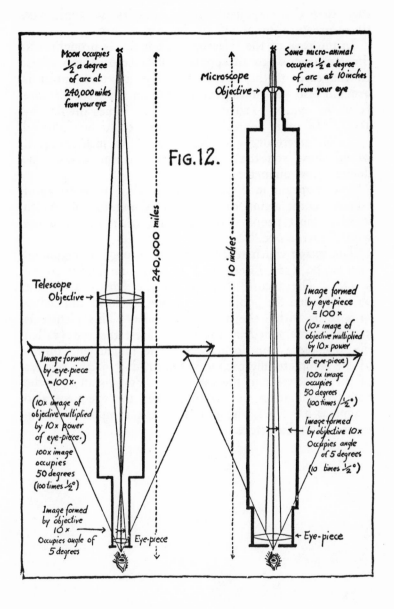

Moon occupies ½ a degree of arc at 240,000 miles from your eye

Microscope Objective →

Some micro-animal occupies ½ a degree of arc at 10 inches from your eye

FIG. 12.

240,000 miles

10 inches

Telescope Objective →

Image formed by eye-piece = 100 ×

(10× image of objective multiplied by 10× power of eye-piece.)

100× image occupies 50 degrees (100 times ½°)

Image formed by objective 10× Occupies angle of 5 degrees

Eye-piece

Image formed by eye-piece = 100 ×

(10× image of objective multiplied by 10× power of eye-piece)

100× image occupies 50 degrees (100 times ½°)

Image formed by objective 10× Occupies angle of 5 degrees (10 times ½°)

← Eye-piece

each case the magnified image occupies an angle 100 times greater—or about 50 degrees of arc.

In the case of the telescope, the moon is brought 100 times nearer, or to an apparent distance of 2,400 miles. In the case of the microscope, the micro-organism is brought also 100 times nearer, or to an apparent distance from the eye of 1/10 of an inch (10 inches divided by 100). In other words, if your eye could be focussed upon the micro-organism at 1/10 of an inch away, it would show you the same image that the microscope does at 100 diameters.

The diagram in *Figure 12* will also serve to show you the construction of a compound microscope, which is what most people have in mind when they use the word "microscope."

The image which reaches the eye through a compound microscope (see *Figure 12*) is really an image of an image. The picture formed by the lens nearest the object (called the "objective") is upside down and comes to a focus within the microscope tube. This picture is in turn re-magnified by the lens nearest the eye (called the "eye-piece" or "ocular"). The magnifying power of the complete microscope is the product of the powers of the objective and the eye-piece. For instance, if the objective magnifies 10 diameters and the eye-piece also magnifies 10 times, the power of the compound instrument is 100 diameters.

III
HOW TO CHOOSE AND HANDLE YOUR WEAPONS FOR HUNTING IN THE MICRO-JUNGLE

No experienced hunter would place a loaded shotgun in the hands of a person who had never fired one, and turn him loose in the woods. Accordingly, the first step in guiding you into the really thrilling pastime sport of hunting with the compound microscope will be a few words about the cautions to exercise in selecting and using one. You are already familiar with the use of the "hand" or "pocket" lens and its possibilities.

The great popularity of the microscope as a hobby has brought a great many instruments of all prices upon the market These are sold both singly and in the form of sets—including a microscope and various accessories in the form of a boxed outfit.

Some of these microscopes have merit, and others are mere toys—utterly useless. The lenses of the latter are so poorly ground that they will not give you a clear image at any magnification. To make them was a waste of time and material, and to give them to a boy or girl as an introduction to the pleasures of microscope-hunting is a crime.

Most of these toy instruments are so bad optically that their use is very hard on the eyes. But this is not their worst feature, for a boy or girl will quickly give up using such a poor instrument, thus removing this danger. The real offense in marketing such an "imitation" of a microscope is that the person who uses it in the freshness of his first enthusiasm is deeply disappointed, and naturally feels that the pleasures of microscope hunting have been much exaggerated. A worthless instrument thus frequently blocks the first eager steps in the path to a hobby which, with even a fairly good microscope, might give both fun and instruction in increasing measure.

As in purchasing any other equipment, you must not believe that you can secure something good for too little. If you pay enough, you can generally be sure of getting a good instrument. But this book is intended to make the microscope hobby as widely enjoyed as possible, and few people can purchase upon this "millionaire's principle." How little, then, can you pay, and still secure a microscope with lenses which will give you clear, sharp views of microscopic life and other objects—and with mechanical adjustments which will be easy and smooth in operation?

There are now microscopes of this quality on the market for as low as $15. This is the least you can pay for a new instrument that is worth using. However, if you look about in places where second-hand goods are sold, or buy from a friend, you may be able to do a little better. A second-hand instrument is just as good as a new one, provided that the adjustments work smoothly, and that the lenses are not scratched. Look very carefully at the visible surfaces of the objective lens and the eye-piece lens and do not purchase if they are scratched in any way.

In cleaning the lenses of your microscope never use anything but a soft, clean handkerchief, or, better still, get some "lens tissue," which is made especially for the purpose. Never touch a lens with your finger tips or clean with a soiled rag.

The ideal microscope for the amateur who expects to take his hobby seriously is a student's microscope with "standard" size objective. (See *Figure 13.*) The size of the screw-thread which fastens the objective upon the lower end of the tube was agreed upon by an international society of microscope makers. Accordingly, if you have a microscope with the standard "society" screw, you can

36

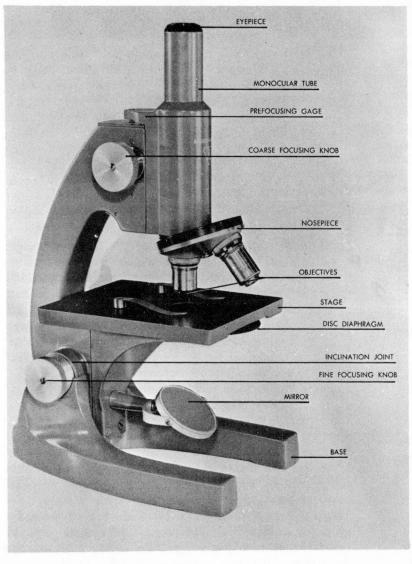

EYEPIECE

MONOCULAR TUBE

PREFOCUSING GAGE

COARSE FOCUSING KNOB

NOSEPIECE

OBJECTIVES

STAGE

DISC DIAPHRAGM

INCLINATION JOINT

FINE FOCUSING KNOB

MIRROR

BASE

Fig. 13. Parts of a compound microscope.

Courtesy of Bausch & Lomb, Rochester N. Y.

acquire objectives of higher power as you need them and can afford to purchase them.

To start with, you can get along very well with two objectives—a low-power one which gives about 50 or 60 diameters magnification and a higher-power one which gives 100 to 120 diameters. The lower-power one will have a focus of about an inch; the higher a focus of about half an inch.

A student's microscope with standard "society" screw objectives can be bought from microscope supply houses for about $60, used. If you can afford to spend this much, it will prove a better purchase than the $15 instrument, because its power can be added to at any time by adding an objective giving greater magnification (of shorter focus) and you can be sure that any modern objective you are able to pick up (perhaps even in a pawnshop) will fit the standard screw thread. The smaller instruments (selling at the minimum price quoted) are furnished with smaller objectives than the "standard." For even this, however, you can secure additional ones of higher power.

How a compound microscope magnifies has already been explained in Chapter 2, but may be summarized while we are talking about objectives and eye-pieces.

For example, an objective of about ½ inch focus (say 16 millimeters) magnifies an object about 10 diameters when used as a magnifier in the hand. When screwed upon the lower end of the microscope tube, the 10-diameter image it makes is thrown above, high up in the tube. Here this image acts in turn as an "object" for magnification by the "eye-piece" or "ocular" at the upper end of the tube. Oculars are made of various strengths—10x, 12x, 15x. With a 10x eye-piece, the 10x objective gives you a magnification of 100x. The 15x eye-piece will make the same objective give an enlargement of 150 diameters, and so on.

Another example: A one-eighth inch objective (focus

about 4 millimeters) gives an initial magnification of about 40 diameters. With a 10x eye-piece, this will give you an enlargement of 400x—which is more than you will need for some time, and as great a power as you will ever need for amateur work. You can look forward to acquiring this ⅛-inch objective if you get a microscope having a "standard" objective screw.

You can still further increase the power of both objective and eye-piece by pulling up the extension draw-tube that most microscopes have in the top of the barrel which moves up and down.

Do not go in too soon for the use of extremely high powers, for they require the experience in handling which can only be gained through doing a lot of observing with the lower powers. Besides, the best microscope is the one which will show you the most detail with the least magnification.

A few words of caution about focusing your instrument should be added. Here they are: *Never focus downward toward the slide containing the object;* always move the objective downward while you are looking at it. *Then focus upward* while you are looking *through* it. If you reverse the process, you will sometime smash a valuable objective through a cover glass, and perhaps scratch it badly. This is not so likely when using a one-inch objective, but it can happen easily with a one-quarter-inch one—and the shorter the focus, the more expensive to replace!

While speaking of objectives, it may be well to mention the "multiple nose-piece." (See *Figure 13.*) It is merely a revolving piece of metal into which two or three objectives can be screwed, ready to be brought one by one into line with the microscope tube. It enables you to change objective powers instantly, without the trouble of unscrewing one and screwing in another. It is, however, not an essential but rather a desirable convenience.

You will soon find that the amount of light which you send up through your microscope by means of the mirror (See *Figure 13*) has a great deal to do with the clearness of your microscopic vision. If your mirror has two sides (a flat and a concave) you can in general use the flat side, although the concave one gives more light. Also in using artificial light, do not use a lamp bulb of too powerful wattage. A frosted bulb of 10 watts (or less, if obtainable), placed several inches away from the mirror, gives enough illumination for practically all purposes. Experiment until you discover the best way to arrange your lamp and mirror.

This arrangement may vary sometimes with the object you are observing. Often the effect is better, and the details clearer, if the mirror is swung to one side, and the rays sent up obliquely through the slide that carries the object. You may, in fact, swing the mirror out of use entirely, and focus rays of light upon the object from above—using a reading glass or other lens held steady by some improvised support. This arrangement is often good for living objects, particularly when a piece of black paper is slipped under the well-slide containing the specimens in their tiny "pond" of water under a cover glass. The objects then stand out brilliantly against a black background.

If your microscope is provided with a "substage condenser" having an iris diaphragm, you will have still another means of controlling and varying the amount of light illuminating your objects. A condenser is simply a lens of very short focus which gathers the light reflected up from the mirror and concentrates it more intensely upon the tiny object being viewed.

Some people are afraid that the eyes may be injured by using a microscope regularly. There is no reason to fear this, provided that a *good* microscope is used. A poorly made toy, with which a clear, sharp view is impossible, will naturally strain the eyes, just as badly fitted spectacles will. However, when using a good, clear instrument, with reasonable precautions, no strain need be felt.

Of course an excess of light should be avoided at all times, and the object should be brought into focus clearly before being examined intently for details. Also, it will be better if you can form the habit of looking through the microscope with both eyes open. After a little practise, the eye which is not looking through the instrument will stop reporting what it sees. If you have trouble at first in forming the both-eyes-open habit, cut a hole in a screen of black card-board and force it over the eye-piece and a little way down the microscope's tube. This will block the vision of the eye not being used for observing.

Any microscope which is intended for serious laboratory work is provided with what is called a "fine adjustment" for careful focusing—in addition to the "coarse" adjustment which they all have. (See *Figure 13.*)

Since we are planning to "bring back alive" the strange wild animals we capture in the pond, we must now give some attention to a means of keeping them alive and well while we are examining them under the lens of our instrument.

HOW TO MAKE AND USE A WELL-SLIDE

We cannot simply run the drop or two of water (containing a tiny bit of green filament and perhaps our tiny menagerie) upon a glass slip and cover it with a cover glass for, even as small as they are, the weight of the cover glass is sufficient to crush and ruin many of the creatures which we will find the most interesting of all to watch. Accordingly, we must provide some sort of a miniature "pond" in which they can swim about freely.

This is easily accomplished by obtaining, or making,

a "well-slide." (See *Figure 14.*) You can buy two kinds of these from dealers in microscopic supplies. One has a depression ground out of the slide itself. In the other the "well" is formed by a pierced piece of glass cemented upon a glass slide. The latter is the better, but the more expensive. However, there is no need for buying either kind ready-made, for you can make as many well-slides as you need by cementing pierced squares of card-board upon slides, using ordinary shellac as an adhesive. The shellac waterproofs the card-board.

If you work in a warm room, you will notice that the water rapidly evaporates around the edges of the cover-glass which covers the well containing your menagerie. To prevent this, keep a small saucer or glass of water handy, containing a tiny camel's hair brush. With this brush you can occasionally add a drop of water at the edge of the cover-glass. Then the capillary attraction of the water will draw it under the cover-glass and replace the water lost by evaporation.

A still better way of taking care of this trouble is to cut off the top of a tiny apothecary's vial with a file, and cement the bottom of the vial to the corner of your well-slide. When this little reservoir is supplied with water and a wick of soft cotton string, it will carry water automatically to the edge of the cover-glass and replace the evaporation without attention from you. (See *Figure 14.*)

HOW TO KEEP SPECIMENS OVERNIGHT

Sooner or later in your hunting adventures you are sure to come across some specimen so beautiful that you will want to keep it for study on the following day, or to show some one else who doesn't happen to be within call when the discovery is made.

If you return the water containing the wonderful specimen to the aquarium or pond-water bottle, it will be lost. What to do?

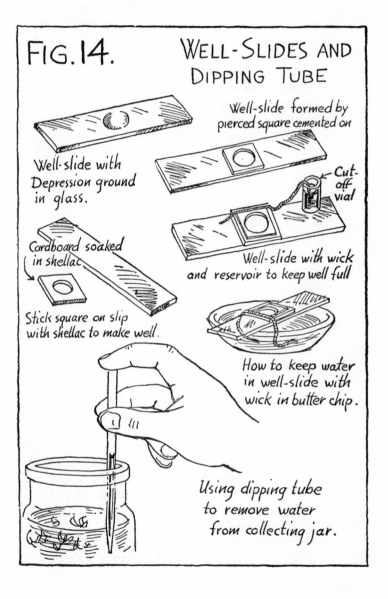

FIG. 14.

WELL-SLIDES AND DIPPING TUBE

Well-slide with Depression ground in glass.

Well-slide formed by pierced square cemented on

Cardboard soaked in shellac

Stick square on slip with shellac to make well.

Cut-off vial

Well-slide with wick and reservoir to keep well full

How to keep water in well-slide with wick in butter chip.

Using dipping tube to remove water from collecting jar.

One of the sketches in *Figure 14* shows the simple procedure which will enable you to set the well-slide aside and keep your specimen in good condition for several days. Simply lay the slide, covered with its cover-glass, across a common butter chip, filled with water, and lay a bit of cotton wick across along the edge of the cover-glass, with both ends of the wick hanging into the water below. The wick will constantly draw up fresh water for the tiny creatures, and the capillary attraction will supply it to them under the thin square of crystal glass.

HOW TO MAKE AND USE A DIPPING TUBE

Another simple device which you will soon find indispensable is the "dipping tube." (See *Figure 14.*) This is just a piece of narrow glass tubing a few inches long with the end drawn down a little smaller than the original size. Get a piece of quarter-inch glass tubing from the drug store and you can make two dipping tubes in a few minutes over the kitchen gas stove. Just heat the middle of the tubing gradually in one of the gas flames until it is red-hot and begins to soften. Then it is easy to draw the two halves apart until the center is narrowed down enough. Then, when cool, snap the two halves apart and your dipping tubes are complete.

To use, proceed as shown in the sketch in *Figure 14.* Place the forefinger firmly over the top of the tube and plunge the lower end into the water of the aquarium or pond-water bottle. Then, as you remove your finger, some of the water will rush up into the tube. When this occurs, replace your finger on the upper opening, and you can dip out the enclosed water, transferring it to a well-slide by again releasing the finger from the upper opening of the dipping tube.

Sometimes you will wish to capture a small "water flea" or some other creature which is just visible to your eye. You can see him moving about in the aquarium. To catch him for observation, proceed as above, except that after plunging the dipping tube into the water, you follow the creature's movement with the lower end of the tube, keeping its opening directly above him. Then suddenly remove the finger from the upper end, and the water flea may rush into your tube with the current of water. If he doesn't, try again. Then you can remove him to a well-slide for observation.

In observing live creatures you will notice that they frequently move out of the field you are looking at, and "leave you flat." To follow them you will need to become expert in moving the slide about on the microscope stage without removing your eye from the eye-piece. This will be confusing at first, for the field moves in the opposite direction to which you move the slide. You will soon catch the knack, however.

FIELD OBSERVATIONS WITH A WELL-SLIDE

If you like to hike, you can have a great deal of pleasure in summer by taking a well-slide, cover-glasses and a dipping tube with you in a little card-board box, along with a pocket lens magnifying 10 or 12 diameters. Transfer a few drops of water from a promising spot among the weeds along the pond shore to your well-slide and examine under a cover-glass with your pocket lens. You can see many of the larger creatures and in time you can learn to detect the presence of creatures as small as *Vorticellae*. When you do this, wash off the water containing them into your collecting bottle, and you may recapture them later.

There is a variety of fountain pen microscope which is very useful on field trips. It is adjustable, and gives magnification of about 30, 40 and 60 diameters. In fact, another model gives over 100. Used in connec-

tion with a well-slide on a hiking trip it will give a lot
of fun to several people who can look in turn at the
specimens discovered in the pond water.

Little need be said about the regular flat glass slips
and thin cover glasses, for every optical store which sells
microscopes also supplies these little accessories. You
will find, however, epecially for observing live creatures
in the well-slide, that the one-inch square cover glasses
are the most convenient and easily handled. Microscope
dealers also carry small bottles of "Canada Balsam,"
a sticky resinous liquid which microscopists use for mount-
ing objects permanently under cover glasses on slips.
It may be worth mentioning here that when an object
is thus permanently mounted upon a "slip" the "slip"
thereupon becomes a "slide."

HOW TO MOUNT IN BALSAM

To mount any small, dry object (such as a fly's wing),
simply place the object in the center of a glass slip, and
let a drop of Canada Balsam fall upon it. Then place
a clean cover glass upon the drop of balsam and press
down very gently until the balsam spreads out to the
edges of the cover glass. In a few days the balsam will
be hard, and the "slide" can be labeled and kept
indefinitely.

HOW TO "DEHYDRATE" SPECIMENS

Do not try, however, to mount in this way any object
which contains water (such as a fly's tongue) for it will
quickly dry up and spoil. Objects containing water must
first be gradually dehydrated (have their water removed)
by soaking in alcohol and water of gradually increasing
strength, and eventually in pure alcohol. Then after a

few hours soaking in turpentine, to increase their transparency, they may be mounted as described above, in Canada Balsam. A mount prepared in this way will remain unchanged.*

HOW TO MAKE A SCOOP-NET

For collecting microscopic specimens, you will often find it convenient to have a little conical net on a ring fastened at the end of a stick. Make a ring of stiff wire with the ends twisted together and bind with waxed string or wire to the end of an ordinary yardstick or half-inch dowel-rod. The ring need be only five or six inches in diameter. Sew on to it a conical bag made from any fine-meshed, thin cloth. An old fine linen or cotton handkerchief is good.

This net can be used for scooping up floating water plants or for catching swimming insects. It has many uses, which will suggest themselves as the occasion arises.

When the net has hauled in its catch of weeds or objects, it can be held over the wide-mouthed collecting bottle or Mason jar and turned inside out into the water in the jar.

And now we have finished with the necessary "technical" advice (somewhat boring, but which seems indispensable to make a success of any hobby) and are ready for the really fascinating part of microscope work—the actual finding and identification of the microscopic plants and animals. The pictures in the following chapters show the varieties which will be most frequently met with by hunters in the micro-jungle of the pond.

---

* In dehydrating begin with 30 per cent alcohol (1 oz. alcohol to 2 oz. water). Leave the specimen about five minutes in this strength; then transfer to 50 per cent alcohol; then to 70, then to 90, and finally to 100 per cent, leaving the object five minutes in each dilution. By having several small bottles you can use the same solutions of alcohol over and over. Eventually, of course, they will all be weakened by the water extracted from your specimens.

IV

WHERE AND HOW TO HUNT
MICROSCOPIC BIG GAME

Many a person has failed to find the pleasure that there is in the possession of a good microscope simply because he, or she, lacked a few simple directions about where to secure a supply of constantly new and really interesting objects for observation.

All too frequently somebody, fascinated by advertising which offers a microscope as the gateway to a world of wonder, blindly buys an instrument, with perhaps a few prepared "slides" of various objects. He looks with natural curiosity at the "tongue of a fly," the "foot of a spider," the "sting of a bee," and perhaps a "section of cornstalk." But he cannot go on looking at these indefinitely—especially as he is not helped in any way to understand what he is seeing. Accordingly, after a few days, the novelty of the new toy is worn off and it is put away, to be eventually sold or forgotten.

How different the story might be if every person who comes into possession of a fairly good microscope could learn at the start that a little vegetable matter from the bank of the nearest pond will furnish an inexhaustible wealth of fascinating *live* objects! Then, instead of discarding the microscope as devoid of interest after his first curiosity was satisfied, he would go on and develop it into a fascinating and perhaps life-long recreation.

And in few other recreations is the first cost almost the only cost, for the ponds or swamps are ready to furnish the microscope hobbyist, once he finds himself with a good instrument, with constantly new and endlessly interesting specimens for the mere trouble of going out and floating a little green vegetable matter into a wide-mouthed bottle, along with some of the surrounding water. Even a teaspoonful of it may furnish a delightful menagerie, large and varied enough to keep one pleasurably amazed for a whole week of evenings.

To furnish a complete guide to all the creatures which may be found in one summer's leisure-time examination of pond water is infinitely beyond the scope of this small book. At the end, a few other books will be mentioned which will enable you to go farther with the subject. In this book I can only mention briefly a few of the most frequently found microscopic creatures, and give you pictures which will enable you to recognize them when they appear under your microscope's objective.

But first it is necessary to point out the most likely hunting grounds where the microscopic pond creatures can be captured—the pastures where they graze most frequently.

To begin with, there is no more likely jungle for the microscopic hunter than a little of the tangled mass of hair-like green filaments which you will find floating loosely in the water at the edge of almost any summer pond. It may look almost repulsive—like slime in fact—but it is really a most clean and beautiful plant. You will agree when you have seen it under the microscope. Accordingly, loosen a little of it with your fingers, while the mass is still floating in the pond, and slip it over the tip of a small wide-mouthed bottle, letting water follow until the bottle is half-full. You should avoid lifting the green filaments *out* of the water before putting into the bottle, for many of your most desirable microscopic specimens may thus be dripped off with the water.

In addition to these green filamentous plants, called *Algae* or *Confervae,* there are a number of other larger varieties of water plants which frequently shelter quantities of the microscopic animals we are hunting.

A few of the most common of these plants are drawn simply in *Figure 15*. In collecting them the same precaution given for *Confervae* should be observed: namely, to float parts of the plants directly into your collecting bottle without lifting them clear of the water.

Most of these aquatic plants have narrow, finely divided leaves, between which it is easy for our extremely small prey to shelter themselves. Find any of the following plants and you will be practically sure to find interesting and greatly varied living objects for your microscope. But it will always be a lottery: you may find a beautiful specimen of a certain creature one day and then not see another for a long time. You may find great numbers of the same kind, or scarcely any two alike. This constant surprise of discovery is what makes pond water jungle-hunting such fun.

Now for a few comments upon the pictures in *Figure 15*, which will enable you to identify the principal pond plants. In doing this, float a single leaf of the plant in a white butterdish, and compare it with the pictures in *Figure 15*.

Do not let the scientific names "stump" you. It is much better to learn the correct titles at once, as some of them have no popular names. Besides, if you know the scientific name, every other micro-hobbyist will know at once what you mean. Botanists give much thought to finding a name which belongs exactly to a given species and no other, so why not use it? To use the correct scientific terms for everything connected with your hobby is a mark of efficiency and an orderly mind.

RANUNCULUS AQUATILIS

(*A* in *Figure 15.*) This plant grows under water in ponds and slow streams. The leaves, which divide

FIG. 15.

WATER PLANTS
on which micro-animals are found

A
Ranunculus
Aquatilis

B
Nymphaea
Odorata

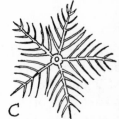

C
Myriophyllum

D
Utricularia
Vulgaris

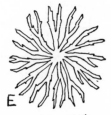

E
Ceratophyllum

F
Lemna and
Lemna Minor

G
Anacharis
Canadensis

H
Sphagnum
Moss

I
Riccia
Fluitans

repeatedly as shown, offer shelter to many microscopic animals, among which you are most likely to find *Rotifers, Vorticellas,* and *Stentors.* (See Chapter 5.) The *Ranunculus* grows entirely under water except for its flower. When blooming, a single white blossom like a butter-cup is lifted above the surface.

NYMPHAEA ODORATA

White Water Lily. (*B* in *Figure 15.*) Since everybody knows this plant at sight, I have drawn a picture of a thin slice of its stem as it appears under a strong pocket lens or low-power of the microscope. It makes a very interesting object when cut very thin with a sharp knife.

As a haunt for microscopic creatures, the *Nymphaea* should be examined carefully with a pocket lens on the under surface of the leaves and along the leaf-stem. If you find any little lumps of jelly or other minute objects adhering to the leaf surface, cut out the bit of leaf that carries the object and examine it under a low power of your microscope.

MYRIOPHYLLUM

(*C* in *Figure 15.*) The leaves of this plant grow in whorls around the central stem, as shown in the picture— which shows a section of stem with a single whorl. When you find *Myriophyllum* growing, you will find it in long green streamers, round and thick. When lifted out of the water they seem almost like ropes. Cut off a small piece in the water and float into your bottle as already described. Another plant somewhat similar to *Myriophyllum* is called *Proserpinaca.* Either of these may be the haunt of many interesting micro-animals.

(*D* in *Figure 15.*) This water plant is easily known by the presence ot the little seed-like bladders, which give it its popular name, "Bladder-wort." These bladders are actually "stomachs," in which small water creatures are trapped and digested by the plant. The microscope hunter's main interest is, however, in the tiny organisms which may frequently be found clinging between its finely divided leaves. Clip off a small portion of one of these and place under a low-power objective.

CERATOPHYLLUM DEMERSUM

(*E* in *Figure 15.*) At first glance you may mistake this plant for *Myriophyllum*, but the likeness will no longer fool you if you cut off a single whorl and compare it with the pictures. You will then see that *Ceratophyllum* is coarser-leaved and rather stiff. Its name, in fact, means "horny-leaved." Also, little spines appear along the leaves. In examining it for possible creatures, cut off only a small piece and put in a "well-slide" filled with water. This plant is found in thick masses, in quiet shallow places in ponds or slow streams.

LEMNA POLYRRHIZA AND LEMNA MINOR

(*F* in *Figure 15.*) The rather silly popular name for this beautiful little floating plant is "duck-meat." It means nothing, as ducks do not eat it, or have anything to do with it. Each plant of *Lemna Polyrrhiza* is made up of little roundish green fronds as shown in the picture. The under-surfaces are a dull purple in color and from them several little white rootlets hang down into the water. The whole plant is hardly over a quarter of an inch across, but in summer large ponds are often covered with them, as with a carpet. Snip off a bit of one of the rootlets, and examine it in a well-slide

53

under your microscope. You may be rewarded with sight of some fine *Vorticellas*, or perhaps *Hydras*, which are fond of perching there too. It is also a good hunting ground for finding *Rotifers*.

Lemna Minor is similar, except that the leaf-fronds are more oval and smaller. Also, their under surfaces are not purple, and have only one rootlet to each frond. Look for the same kind of creatures as on the larger *Lemna*.

ANACHARIS CANADENSIS

(*G* in *Figure 15.*) This plant grows under water, in long stems, which are surrounded by whorls of three leaves each, as shown in the picture. The leaves and stems are semi-transparent and rather tender, breaking easily. The spaces between the leaves are frequently shelters for many *Hydras,* but almost any other micro-animals may be found there too.

SPHAGNUM MOSS

(*H* in *Figure 15*) In this picture (as in *B* also) a magnified section is shown, rather than the complete plant. Note the water-holding spaces between the cells of the plant. The ability of this moss to hold water makes it very useful to florists who use it to pack live plants for shipment. The moss grows on the wet shores of shady bogs and swamps. Its principal interest for the microscope hobbyist is that it may be covered with *Infusoria, Rhizopoda, Diatoms* and *Desmids,* which will wash off in the water when a bit of moss is put in a well-slide and examined under the objective.

RICCIA FLUITANS

(*I* in *Figure 15.*) This plant grows in paper-thin green ribbons, sometimes an inch or more wide. It grows in long, branching strands, without roots, floating in the water. Like the other plants in this chapter, a bit of the leaf should be snipped off, put in a well-slide, and examined for any creatures which may be attached to it.

These few plants are the principal sources of micro-animals to be encountered in ponds and slow streams, but almost any bit of water vegetation is worth putting to the test of the microscope. You never know when even a sixteenth of an inch of a green water plant will bring you the sight of some unsuspected marvel of the miniature world.

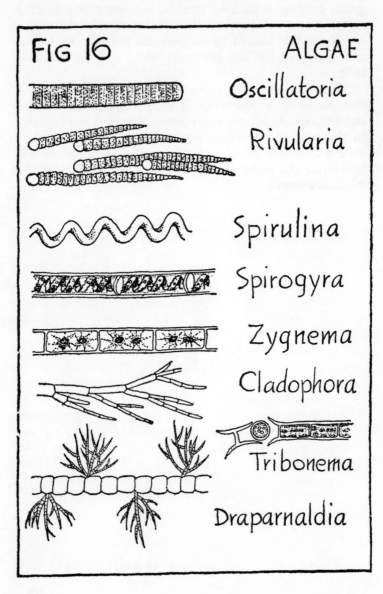

FIG 16   ALGAE

Oscillatoria

Rivularia

Spirulina

Spirogyra

Zygnema

Cladophora

Tribonema

Draparnaldia

V

WHAT TO LOOK FOR WITH THE MICROSCOPE

THE SMALLER PLANTS OF THE MICRO-JUNGLE

When you enter the domain of the infinitely small in the water world, it becomes extremely difficult to tell plants from animals. In fact, over some of its denizens the scientific battle has raged for years. Plant? Or animal? And it is not surprising, for in the microscopic jungle some of the smaller plants move about looking for food quite as freely as do the animals.

PLANTS ARE GREEN——BUT NOT ALWAYS

However, there is one test that holds in the water world just as well as it does on dry land. On our walks in the fields and woods we generally feel fairly safe in identifying plants by their green color, and this is also a reasonably certain identifying feature in two of the three classes of tiny plants which appear in the fields of our microscope.

In this and the succeeding chapters we are going to follow the same plan that we did in the chapter on the subjects for the pocket lens: supply you with many pictures to help you recognize and name what you see, and make passing comments on those objects about which we know interesting little bits of gossip.

The three chief classes of microscopic plants are called *Algae, Desmids,* and *Diatoms.* The *Algae* and *Desmids* always show the green plant coloring-matter which we call "chlorophyl," but the *Diatoms* are apt to be as brown as the mud where they are frequently found.

A FEW OF THE "ALGAE"

(*Figure 16.*)   The masses of long, stringy, green

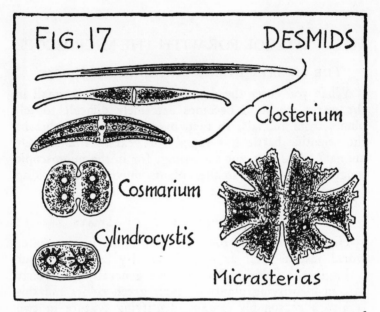

FIG. 17   DESMIDS

Closterium

Cosmarium

Cylindrocystis

Micrasterias

filaments which float in clouds in shallow water, and feel like sodden felt when lifted out, are made up of the most plentiful species of the water plants that we call *Algae*. On the whole, the *Alga* family tends to be long, stringy and filamentous, but not invariably.

In *Figure 16,* I have selected and drawn a few of the *Algae* which you are most likely to meet with, and have tagged them with names almost as hard to pronounce and remember as those of some of our equally common garden shrubs and plants. You will find the beautiful form called *Spirogyra* especially interesting, with its ribbon-like band of green chlorophyll twisting round and round.

Of course, you will never find a single variety of any-thing, plant or animal, alone. A few filaments of *Spiro-gyra,* for instance, may have lovely little colonies of *Vorticellae,* or Bell Flower Animalcules, hanging to them,

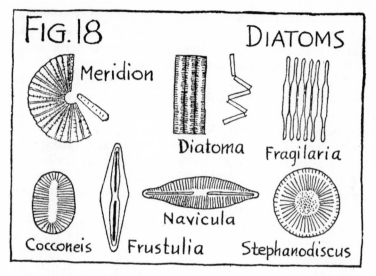

FIG. 18   DIATOMS

Meridion

Diatoma   Fragilaria

Cocconeis   Frustulia   Navicula   Stephanodiscus

while all around swim *Rotifers*, *Volvox* and other creatures—a veritable menagerie. However, the only way we can show you what the individual plants and animals look like is to exhibit them in our pictures as they never are in real life—namely, classified. This book has to make a few concessions to systematic science.

THE SYMMETRICAL DESMIDS

(*Figure 17.*) While the members of the *Alga* family tend to form long strings of cells, the beautiful green *Desmids* are all single-celled. They tend to appear in balanced halves. These microscopic plants generally adhere to the stems and leaves of larger water plants, such as those described in Chapter 3.

THE HARD-SHELLED DIATOMS

(*Figure 18.*) These pictures represent a very few of one of the strangest families of plants that ever existed—the *Diatoms*. From their shapes you would never even guess that they were plants, and when you learn that each Diatom lives incased in a hard, stone pill-box of a case you wonder how they live at all.

You will find Diatoms practically everywhere that there is mud and water. Smudge a little mud from the pond-shore on a glass slip and the microscope will be likely to show on it several Diatoms—perhaps a great many.

Smear a little tooth paste on a slide and examine it. Here also, if the tooth paste is made from chalk, you will be likely to find the fossil skeletons of Diatoms, millions and billions of which helped to make up the world's chalk deposits.

Diatoms are highly geometric in form—circles, ovals, triangles—all with patterns as precise as if laid out with mechanical drawing instruments. Many are beautifully and regularly decorated with lines of dots, parallel ribs or spines. The pictures give only a hint of their variety: there are over 1,200 species.

Animals with Roots for Feet and with Whips for Propellers—and a Garden of Flower-Animals

AMOEBA AND ITS COUSINS

If, when looking through your microscope at water life, you see what looks like a tiny dab of colorless jelly, watch it for a moment or two. It may extend a part of its main body into a rather shapeless arm or leg, (call it a "root" if you like) which may eventually be drawn back into the body again. If you see this happen, you will probably be watching an *amoeba*—the simplest member of the family which have been named the "rhizopods," or the "root-footed" creatures. (From *rhizo,* "root" and *pod* "foot.") You will look upon an amoeba with more respect if you remember that he represents the ancestor of every animal, fish and bird living on

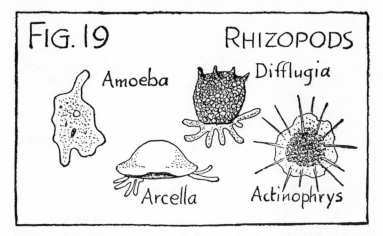

FIG. 19   RHIZOPODS

Amoeba   Difflugia

Arcella   Actinophrys

earth. All life came first from a single-celled, formless beginning like this creature you see slowly changing its shape under the lens. See page 102 for more details.

In *Figure 19* I have drawn for you a few of the members of this strange family which you may meet, and have added their names, so that you may be properly introduced to each other when you meet.

INVENTORS OF THE "PULL" PROPELLER

(*Figure 20.*) Some day you may notice in the water scene under your objective a little green ball, apparently containing a few smaller ones inside. The larger ball rolls along through the water without any apparent cause. However, if you get the quantity and direction of your light source arranged just right, you will see that the propelling of the sphere is done by the lashing of many tiny, thread-like whips. You are looking at a Volvox, one of the group of microscopic creatures called the *flagellates,* or "whip-bearers." These creatures are of extraordinary shapes, as you will see from the sketches in *Figure 20,* but they are all related in this one par-

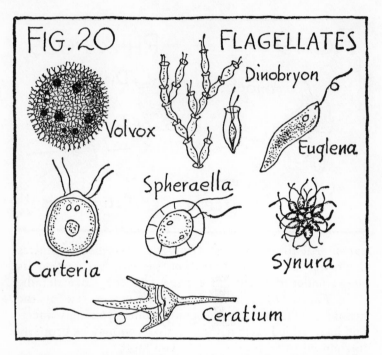

FIG. 20   FLAGELLATES

Volvox

Dinobryon

Euglena

Spheraella

Carteria

Synura

Ceratium

ticular—they lash themselves through the water by the use of whips. The picture which this brings into your mind is of course one in which the creature is propelled by lashing out *behind* it with its whip. This is, however, usually contrary to the method you will observe if you look carefully. You will find that the lash is vibrated *ahead* of the organism, which is pulled after its whip, just as an airplane is driven by being pulled after its propeller.

WHEN ANIMALS BECOME BLOSSOMS

(*Figure 21.*)   Until you have seen a colony of *Vorticellae* (or Bell-Flower Animalcules) you do not know what fascination your microscope is capable of furnish-

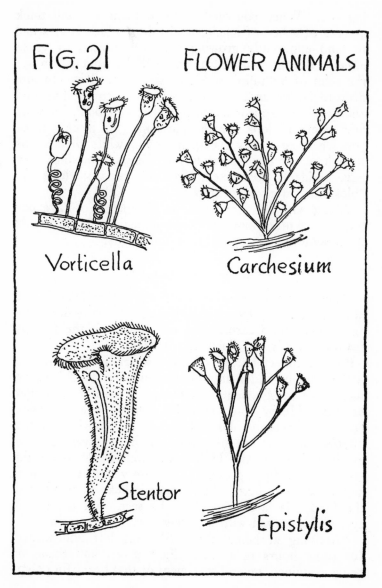

FIG. 21   FLOWER ANIMALS

Vorticella

Carchesium

Stentor

Epistylis

ing you. When you catch sight of them you will think at once of a bed of infinitesimal tulips, which is attached to, and apparently growing out of a thread of green *algae*. But as you watch, you will be amazed to see the stem of a "tulip" suddenly shorten and its blossom drop to the ground. Then this happens to another, and another. It happens so quickly that you don't know at first where to look for the blossoms. It is only when you see them slowly rising up again, while their stems straighten out the "spiral spring" shape into which they have suddenly contracted, that you realize where the "blossoms" went when they vanished.

Along with the *Vorticellae* in *Figure 21*, I have pictured three other kinds of flower animals which resemble them somewhat in appearance and habits.

A CARNIVOROUS PALM-TREE

Another minute creature which you will frequently find attached to things by a stem, although it is very decidedly an animal, and a carnivorous one at that, is the famous fresh-water *Hydra,* illustrated in *Figure 22.*

If you collect bottles of pond water frequently, you will probably find many Hydras sticking to the inside surface of the glass, just as Henry J. Slack relates that he did. Henry Slack was the author of a charming book, "Marvels of Pond Life," first published in the 1870's and now out of print. In it he gives such an excellent idea of the Hydra (as well as of the right way to use a dipping tube) that I am venturing to quote a portion of it here. In reading it bear in mind that the Hydra is large enough to be seen with the naked eye, and observed with a pocket lens. Slack writes:

"Arriving at home, the bottle was left undisturbed for some hours in a warm light place, and then, on being examined, several specimens of that beautiful polyp,

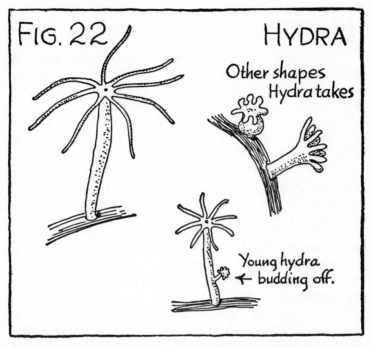

FIG. 22

HYDRA

Other shapes
Hydra takes

Young hydra
← budding off.

the *Hydra Viridis,* were seen attached to the glass, and spreading their delicate tentacles in search of prey. One of the polyps is carefully removed by the *dipping tube,* a small glass tube, open at both ends. The fore-finger is placed upon the top, and when the other end is brought over the object the finger is raised for an instant, and as the water rushes in, the little hydra comes too, and is placed in a glass cell about half an inch wide and one-tenth of an inch deep. After the hydra has been placed in it, a little more water is taken up in the dipping tube, and the cell filled until the fluid stands in a convex heap above its brim. We then select a cover glass and press it gently down upon the walls of our cell. A few drops of superfluous water escape, and we have the cell quite full, and the cover held tight by force of the capillary attraction between the water and the glass.

"The polyp deposited in one of these water-cages is then transferred to the stage of the microscope, and its proceedings watched. At first it looks like a shapeless mass of apple-green jelly. Soon, however, the tail end of the creature is fixed to the glass, the body elongates, and the tentacles (in this case eight) expand something after the manner of a graceful palm.

"By accident two small water-fleas were imprisoned with the polyp, and one (a shrimp-like looking creature, carrying behind her a great bag of eggs) came into contact with the tentacles, and seemed paralyzed for a time. The Hydra made no attempt to convey the captive to his mouth, but held it tight until another water flea, a round, merry little fellow (*Chydorus Sphoericus*), came to the rescue, and assisted *Canthocamptus* to escape by tugging at her tail.

"Watching the Hydra, it was curious to note the changes of form which these creatures are able to assume. Now the tentacles were short and thick, and the body squat. Now the body was elongated, like the stem of a palm tree, and the tentacles hung gracefully from the top. From some of the polyps (clinging to the side of the collecting jar) little round buds were growing, while other buds were already developed into miniature copies of the parent, and were only attached by a slender stalk. In a few days many of these left the maternal side, fixed their own little tails to the glass, and commenced housekeeping on their own account.

"Hydras may be obtained at all times of the year by bringing home duckweed (*Lemna Polyrrhiza*), Conferva (*Algae*) and other water plants from the ponds. Some hauls may be unsuccessful, but if one pond is not propitious others should be tried. The plants should be put into a capacious vessel of water, and placed in the light, where, if polyps are present, they will show themselves within 24 hours, either attached to the sides of the glass, or hanging from the plants, or suspended heads downwards from the upper film of the water. They are elegant objects and may be kept without difficulty for some weeks."

ROTIFERS—THE MICRO-ANIMALS THAT EAT WITH A VENTILATING FAN

In *Figure 23* I have drawn for you the recognizable portraits of a few of the remarkable family of microscopic creatures called "Rotifers," or "wheel-bearers."

The early microscope pioneers discovered them in pond water, just as you will, and were so fascinated by the apparent rotation of the spokes of wheels around the mouths of the animals that no other name would do. They had to be named "wheel bearers," and you will agree with the appropriateness of the name the moment you see a Rotifer's wheel rotating as he perches upon a thread of Algae or swims through the microscopic swamp. To me, however, the motion always suggests the whirling of an electric ventilator such as is placed in the window of a restaurant kitchen to suck out the overheated air. Also this expresses what really is happening in the Rotifer's case, for the motion creates in the water a current which sucks particles of food into the Rotifer's mouth. You know that it is food, because the creature's body is transparent, like glass, and you can see the peculiar "set of teeth" in its throat grinding away for dear life!

Another use for the wheel is that it propels the creature through the water just as the rotating screw-propellor of a motor boat boes.

I am sure that you are extremely doubtful that a

"wheel" can actually be revolving around any creature's mouth, so it may be well to explain that the wheel-appearance is an optical illusion. The appearance of rotation is caused by the rapid bending down and recovering of a circular row of "cilia"—or hairs like your eye-lashes. It is the same illusion that you see in the apparently moving border of an electric sign. The line of light seems to revolve around the sign, but the cause is found in many series of three or four bulbs in a row, which go on and off in rapid succession.

The Rotifers present so many fascinations that I am sure they will at once become your pets out of the entire micro-menagerie, just as they have of generations of microscope hobbyists. One very startling feature of many Rotifers is the "telescopic" tails. The sections actually slide into each other, like the sections of a spy-glass, thus enabling the creature to fold himself up into smaller compass.

Most Rotifers are so active that they give you good practice in moving the slide under the objective without removing your eye from the ocular. However, some of this family are not swimmers at all, but live all their lives in tubular houses which they build and attach to water plants.

One of the most remarkable of these is shown in *Figure 23* over the amazingly girlish name of *Melicerta*. Melicerta is at once brickmaker, mason and architect and builds herself a chimney-like house out of little mud-balls, which she molds one by one, and then adds to the circular wall.

The Melicerta's tubular homes are just large enough to be seen with the naked eye. With your pocket lens you can sometimes find them adhering in groups to the under side of a pond-lily leaf. In this case, clip out the bit of leaf carefully and put into a well-slide of water for observation under pocket lens and microscope. Later,

68

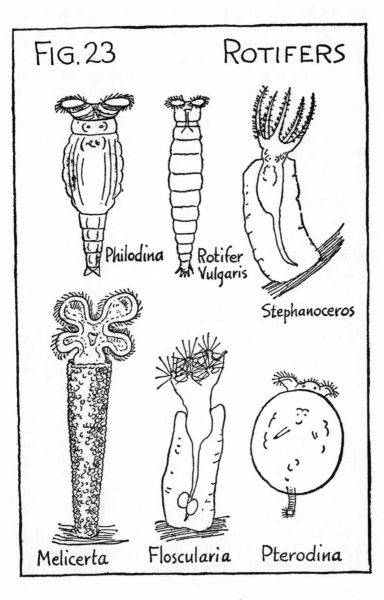

Fig. 23   Rotifers

Philodina

Rotifer Vulgaris

Stephanoceros

Melicerta

Floscularia

Pterodina

put the bit of leaf into a vial of water, and keep the water fresh. In this way a specimen can be preserved alive for several days, and transferred to the well-slide when you want to exhibit *Melicerta* and her brick chimney to admiring friends. If you watch very patiently, you may even see her making bricks and using them to lengthen her house.

So much for the Rotifer family. You will find them fascinating, from the very first glimpse you obtain of the commonest kind, to your final delighted discovery of some of the rarest varieties.

Hunting Water Fleas, a "Water Bear," and Dwellers in Jelly

You can hardly put a drop of pond water into your well-slide for observation without adding a few "water fleas."

You can see these little crustaceans or "micro lobsters" even with your naked eye in a bottle of water collected with water plants. They are those rapidly moving dots which swim so steadily and so tirelessly. Under a low power of your microscope you will recognize the principal varieties quite easily from the sketches I have given you in *Figure 24* .

CYCLOPS IN MINIATURE

Probably the most frequently seen of all is the one called *Cyclops*, with her two little egg bags trailing behind, and the single eye which gives her the name of the one-eyed giant of Greek mythology. It seems odd to give a giant's name to a creature which can hardly be seen with the naked eye!

Another very common one is the creature called *Daphnia*. The dried bodies of this variety are sold in little boxes in aquarium stores as food for gold fish. This

FIG. 24   WATER FLEAS, WATER BEAR AND POLYZOA

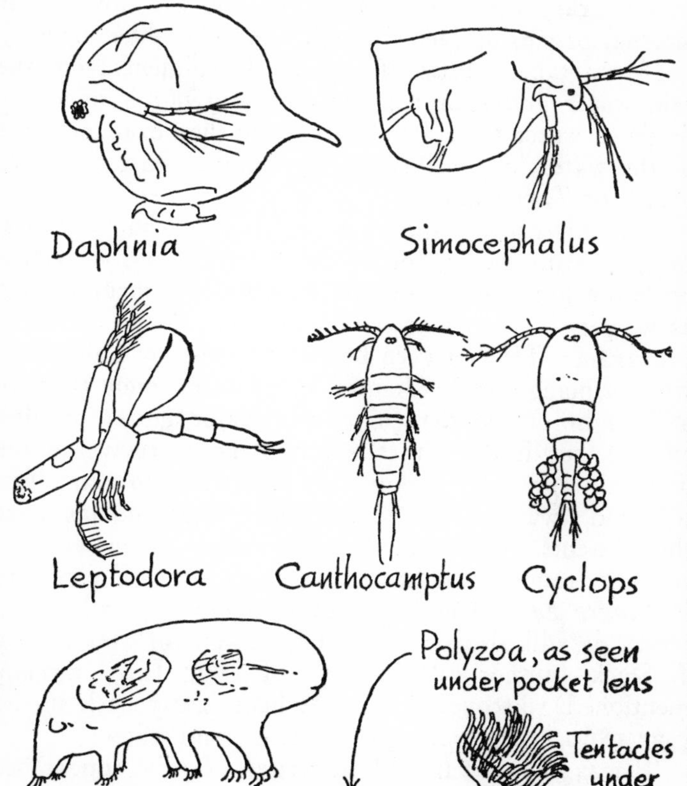

Daphnia

Simocephalus

Leptodora   Canthocamptus   Cyclops

Water Bear

Polyzoa, as seen under pocket lens

Tentacles under microscope.

shows what millions of them there are in every pond in the world, for it takes a lot of microscopic *Daphnia* to weigh an ounce.

ANIMALS IN GLASS HOUSES

The crustaceans or "water fleas" are especially interesting if you can get them to be quiet for a second or two (a rare occurrence) for then you can study their internal organs as seen through their glass-like shells.

If you take a little of the dried sediment from the rain water gutter of a house-roof and put it in a few drops of water for a few hours—and then examine some of the water in a well-slide—you may capture a "water bear," or *Tartigrade*.

This microscopic animal is one of the "toughest" customers in the world, for he can be dried and shrivelled up into a grain of powder for months, and then, as soon as he gets into reviving water, he immediately comes to life again. He can even be heated to 250° Fahrenheit without being killed. He may have lain dormant through a drought of months (in a rain water gutter or elsewhere) but it doesn't take him long to revive in the first rain and start looking for something to eat. You will find "water bears" occasionally when looking over the contents of bottles of pond water. They are not so very frequent, but worth watching for. The picture in *Figure 24* will help you to recognize one when you see it, as will also the following account of how Henry J. Slack (author of "Marvels of Pond Life" already mentioned) discovered a water bear, away back in the year 1860, when looking over some pond water:

"I was soon rewarded," he writes, "by the appearance of a little puppy-shaped animal very busy pawing about with eight imperfect legs, but not making much progress with all his efforts. It was evident that we had obtained one of the *Tardigrada* (slow steppers) or Water Bears,

72

and a very comical amusing little fellow he was. The figure was like that of a new-born puppy; each of the eight legs was provided with four serviceable claws; there was no tail and the blunt head was susceptible of considerable alteration of shape. He was grubbing about among some bits of decayed vegetation, and from the mass of green stuff in his (transparent) stomach it was evident that he was not one of that painfully numerous class in England—the starving poor."

POLYPS IN JELLY

If, when hunting pond material, you should turn over a waterlogged floating stick or sodden chip, and should see a little mass or patch of shining clear or brown jelly, do not throw it away. Instead, examine it carefully with your pocket lens; you may find that you have captured one of the loveliest of microscopic objects—a colony of fresh-water *polyzoa*. The name comes from "poly" (meaning "many") and "zoon" (an animal). It is accordingly, "many animals."

The different "animals" composing a colony look more like miniature flowers as they protrude their petal-like tentacles from the ends of the many-branched tubes of jelly in which they live. (See *Figure 24*.)

These animals are shy at first. When you first pick up the chip or stick on which the jelly-patch is visible, you will probably see nothing of the flower-like appearance, for the animals, in fright, have drawn in their tentacles. But place the bit of wood or bark carrying the colony in a glass of water and watch through a lens. When all is quiet, a crown of little tentacles will be slowly pushed out from each of the branching tubes of jelly.

The best way to observe the *polyzoa* is of course to separate the colony gently from its support (or cut off a little of the support with it) and transfer it to a water-cell on the microscope stage. The tentacles (see *Figure 24*) are then a beautiful sight under a power of 50 or 60 diameters, especially if the light can be arranged to come obliquely from the side, or can be cast from a reading glass held above the water-cell.

Do not be surprised at the size of any colony of *polyzoa* you may find, for occasionally one covers the entire under side of a water-logged plank. The largest I ever heard of covered the entire circumference of an old wagon wheel which had been allowed to float indefinitely in a shady pond in the woods. However, you will find them more often as mere patches on chips, leaves, twigs, and so on.

VI

HOW TO DO MICROSCOPIC DETECTIVE WORK

One of the most fascinating fields which you can enter, with both your pocket lens and your microscope, is the detection of crime!

This does not mean that you can at once start solving murder mysteries, but that you can gradually become expert in detecting such misdemeanors as the adulteration of every day articles like cloth, coffee, flour, tobacco, spices and so on. And who knows but that you will find microscopic detective work so fascinating that you will gradually qualify as an expert in one of its branches that is really indispensable in criminal prosecution!

This chapter will give you several hints in that direction, which you can follow up, if you wish, with the aid of books on these specialties in forensic, or legal microscopy. These hints will include finger-print investigation and the study of forgeries in penmanship. Subjects like these, aside from the interest they possess in themselves, enable you to pursue your hobby at times when pond-life, insects and other nature material is scarce.

IDENTIFYING FIBERS

We will begin with a branch of the micro-detective's work which is far from being despised by the professional criminal investigator—the identification of fibers and hairs.

The appearances of cotton, linen, silk and wool fibers are so characteristic under the microscope that, once you are familiar with them, you can identify them under any circumstances.

To start, pull out threads of each of these materials

from bits of the various textiles, and shred the threads apart with the points of large needles until you have the individual fibers separated. Then put a few of each kind on a separate slide, and become familiar with the appearance of the cotton, linen, silk, and wool fibers—both dry and mounted in water under a cover glass.

Figure 25 shows roughly what to expect in each case, but a few comments will help, and actual experience will soon make you an expert "detective" of these common materials.

If you have a companion in your microscopic researches, you can make a very interesting game of it (after you have both learned to know the fabric fibers) by giving each other "mixed unknowns" a slide on which silk and cotton fibers, for example, are placed in water under a cover glass by one person and handed to the other for identification. By solving these unknowns, you will become a more expert detective than in any other way.

Here are a few comments on *Figure 25* which will help you to know these four fibers to start with. Later, you can extend your knowledge by examining the fibers of many other substances, such as raffia, jute, bamboo, a larger variety of hairs and so on.

Cotton fiber has a flat and twisted appearance, as shown in the sketch. The ribbon-like fiber appears to be thicker and rounded along its edges, and this appearance is explained when we learn that each fiber is really a long collapsed and twisted tube. It is shown in cross-section at (A).

Linen fiber is also a tube, but its walls are so thick that it does not collapse and become a flat ribbon, which makes it easy to tell from cotton. A few linen fibers are shown in cross-section at (B). In addition, you will notice that a linen fiber has frequent small swellings or knobs. The canal in the center is merely a narrow line in the middle of the fiber.

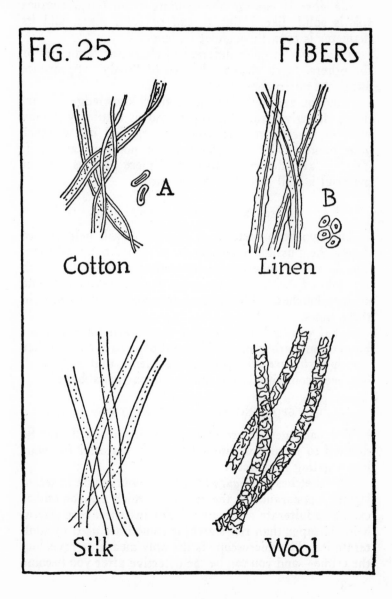

Fig. 25   Fibers

Cotton   A

Linen   B

Silk

Wool

Silk fiber is easy to differentiate from linen, because silk is solid, like a tiny thread of solid glass, and its diameter is even throughout its length.

Wool fiber is quite different in character from any of the others, for it shows a broken or "scaly" appearance under the microscope.

Now you are equipped with enough knowledge to start doing detective work on any unknown textiles you may wish to investigate. If you want to find out whether your handkerchief is really linen or not you can do it. You can also determine whether a piece of dress or suit material is "all wool" or partly cotton.

DETECTING TOBACCO-CHEAPENING

The two little sketches in *Figure 26* will help you to detect the possible adulteration of tobacco by cabbage. The leaves of tobacco are covered with fine hairs which are jointed, with the last joint oval, as shown in one of the sketches. The dust of tobacco is apt to contain these hairs.

But if you find that some of these loose hairs are not jointed, but rather short, thick and pointed (see the other sketch in *Figure 26*) you have evidence that a "crime" has been committed: the tobacco is partly cabbage!

SPOTTING FOOD ADULTERATION

The packages of groceries in the kitchen will now be drafted to furnish additional research material for your investigating microscope.

The sketches in *Figure 27* will be your guide in learning the appearance of the starches, which are sometimes used to adulterate each other. For instance, corn starch, being cheaper than rice starch, is sometimes used to adulterate it. The microscope is the only means of revealing the crime—and you can be the detective after you become

78

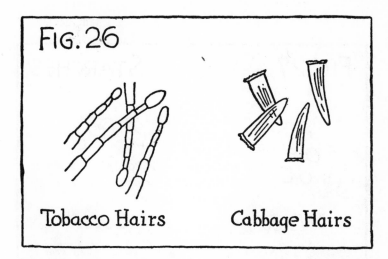

FIG. 26

Tobacco Hairs   Cabbage Hairs

familiar with the actual appearances as indicated in *Figure 27.* Here also a few comments may help.

Wheat starch is made up of small smooth granules, which look like flattened pebbles under the microscope. They are generally somewhat "lenticular" in shape, that is, like a thick double-convex lens.

Corn starch, however, has grains which are "polyhedral," or many-sided in shape, and have small cross-like depressions in their centers.

Rice starch granules are considerably smaller than either wheat or corn, and triangular, square or pentagonal in shape. They are found in larger oval groups, and also scattered individually, or two or three together. The sketch indicates both appearances.

Tapioca starch grains are slightly smaller than corn-starch granules, but nearly round, and have round depressed centers.

Potato starch has the largest granules of any common starch and each particle shows irregular concentric oval rings, as indicated in the sketch.

FIG. 27   STARCHES

Wheat   Corn

Rice   Tapioca

Potato   Bean

FIG. 28 — STRUCTURE OF COFFEE

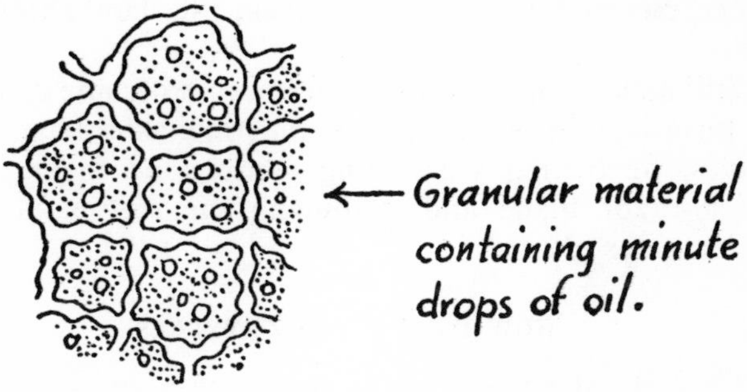

← Granular material containing minute drops of oil.

Bean starch also has the oval concentric rings, but the granules are somewhat smaller, and show several irregular, crack-like markings running outward from the center of each particle.

Ground coffee is another common substance which is sometimes adulterated, so you will find it interesting to know the structure of ground coffee as it looks under the microscope. Its very characteristic appearance is shown in *Figure 28*.

Coffee is made up of a firm network which encloses cells filled with a granular material containing minute drops of oil. The outline of each cell is wavy, owing to irregular swellings in the network surrounding it. The shape of the cells varies somewhat, according as the cell comes from the center of the bean, or nearer the outside, but always contains the oil drops, and the wavy outline. A particle of ground coffee is easy to distinguish under the microscope from chicory (which is its most frequent adulterant) because the chicory has long fibrous cells of the kind common in the stems of plants.

You can also learn some interesting things about the structure of muscle-fibres by shredding out, on individual slides, minute bits of raw beefsteak, fish, lamb, and other meats.

Still another worthwhile series of microscopic structures is furnished by stripping off the thin skin from green leaves, or cutting very thing sections of them with a safety-razor blade and examining the section in water under cover glasses.

HOW TO PREPARE CRYSTALS

Crystals of various kinds constitute a specialty all by themselves. You can begin by evaporating solutions of common chemicals like sugar, salt, cream of tartar, alum, and so on, and examining the resulting microscopic crystals. Just put a few drops of the solution on a clean slide and dry out the water with gentle heat. Then examine, either dry, or mounted in Canada balsam under a coverglass.

BLOOD CELLS AND CHEEK CELLS

An excellent place to begin your study of human blood cells is the tip of your little finger. Page 105 describes in detail how to go about extracting blood from this finger, and preparing it on a slide, for study under your microscope.

Another good source from which to obtain cells is the inside of your cheek. Page 98 contains a full description of a simple method of scraping the inner cheek lining of your mouth, and preparing the scraping for microscopic examination.

In the winter you can also have a lot of fun by taking your microscope out of doors and examining snowflakes caught upon black velvet which has become thoroughly chilled so that the flakes do not melt immediately.

DETECTING POLLEN FROM VARIOUS PLANTS

Another specialty for which extensive use has been found in actual criminal detective work is the classifying of the hundreds of varieties of pollen powder from the stamens of plants.

Under the microscope you will find that the forms of the pollen-grains are almost as sharply differentiated as the flowers of the plants from which the pollen comes. Some are amazingly sculptured, covered with spinous projections, or otherwise characterized.

One case (occurring in France) in which pollen broke down a criminal's alibi will indicate the possibilities of pollen study in detective work.

A murder suspect was arrested far from the scene of the crime, and he brought a witness to prove that he had not been in that district for months.

It was found however that the wax in his ears contained the pollen of a plant which grew only in the section where the crime was committed. Later, the criminal confessed that he had been there and had killed the victim.

A good way to study pollen is to collect the powder in small envelopes and make a permanent mount of each kind in Canada balsam. Label each slide carefully. You will then have a valuable collection of different varieties of pollen for comparison with any unknown which you may wish to identify.

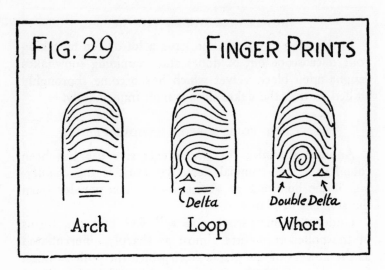

FIG. 29   FINGER PRINTS

Arch   Loop   Whorl

THE A.B.C. OF FINGERPRINTS

This is a vast subject, calling for extensive study with books devoted to the specialty. You can, however, learn enough in a few minutes to begin the examination of fingerprints with a good pocket lens or a low power of your microscope.

Figure 29 indicates the three principal classifications of the designs formed by the papillary ridges on the fingers.

The arch is formed when the ridges cross the finger symmetrically from side to side, gradually curving higher and higher as the tip of the finger is approached.

The loop is formed when the ridges start from one side of the finger and curve back toward the same side. For this case the small triangular area between the bend of the finger and the recurving loops is called a "delta."

The whorl is formed by a spiral near the center of the finger, over which the papillary ridges curve upward. The two small areas on either side of the spiral then form "double deltas."

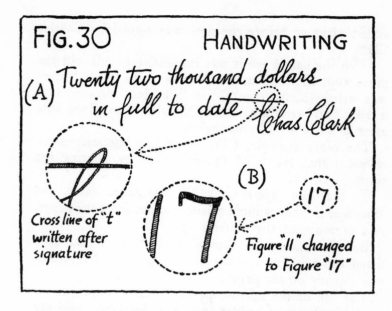

FIG. 30   HANDWRITING

(A) Twenty two thousand dollars in full to date Chas. Clark

Cross line of "t" written after signature

(B)

17

Figure "11" changed to Figure "17"

Upon the foundation of these three simple forms all the complex system of fingerprint identification is based.

DETECTING HANDWRITING FORGERIES

There is hardly a murder trial which does not call for the services of one or more handwriting experts, and the mainstay of every expert is his microscope. Under a magnification of only 50 or 100 diameters even the most perfect forgery of a signature, or alteration in a figure on a check, reveals characteristics which frequently expose its spurious character.

Figure 30 gives two illustrations of the ways in which the microscope proves useful in establishing the genuineness or falsity of "questioned documents."

In example (A) it was required to determine whether the words "in full to date," appearing on a note, were added after or before the note was signed by Charles Clark.

With the naked eye it was impossible to tell, but the microscope showed that the crossing of the "t" in "date" was written across the "C" in "Charles," proving that a crime had been committed by the alteration of the note after it was signed by its maker.

The other example, (B), shows how the microscope revealed that the 7 of 17 was made by altering the second 1 of 11.

To the naked eye the faked 7 was undetectable, and looked as if made without raising the pen from the paper, as a person naturally writes a "7."

But the microscope showed that the pen had been lifted after adding the top of the "7" to a "1" which was already on the paper.

The use of the microscope in detective work has recently made great strides, and has furnished evidence resulting in the punishment of crimes which would have gone scot-free for lack of proof only a few years ago.

DETECTING PAPER MATERIALS

The first paper in the world was the papyrus of the Egyptians—and if it had remained the only paper, we should have no need for studying the various materials with a view to detecting them in unknown samples.

Papyrus was built up from the thin skin of the stems of the papyrus plant. This tissue was peeled off, and the resulting strips were laid crosswise to form woven sheets. After drying under pressure, the papyrus paper was ready to write on with a brush or reed pen. Papyrus was widely used, because it was much cheaper than parchment, the dried skin of animals.

Paper, as we know it today, was invented by the

Chinese. The first material was cotton, but they also used the pulp of mulberry or other woods, straw, and vegetable stems. Linen came into use as paper material in the middle ages and was used in Arabia in 1100 A.D.

The use of wood-pulp from forest trees as material for cheap paper was suggested by the French naturalist Reamur. He had watched wasps building a paper nest from the wood-fibres they scraped from fence posts and other exposed wood, "Why not do likewise?", thought Reamur, and as a result we have modern newspapers and a whole class of cheap magazines called "the pulps."

In the process of making wood pulp paper the finely shredded wood is heated with strong alkali, reduced to a creamy paste and then washed free of the alkali. This semi-liquid wood is then spread out on rollers to a thin sheet, and gradually dried.

Many other materials are also used for various kinds of paper, including corn-husks, straw, sawdust, etc. Accordingly, it often becomes of commercial importance to be able to detect the materials composing any given sample. For this work the microscope is the most important aid.

To prepare paper for microscopic examination first tear it into very small bits, and boil them for a few minutes in a weak (1 per cent) solution of caustic soda. Then wash thoroughly on a fine sieve, and shake the resulting pulp in a test-tube of clean water. From this you can transfer a drop or two of the milky liquid to a slide for examination.

Identification of the materials composing the sample of paper is made by noting the size and shape of the wood-cells, their length, width compared to length, shape of the ends, etc. A few characteristics of the commonest paper materials—wood and straw—now follow.

The trees used for paper materials are of two main

sorts. One kind embraces the pine family, including spruce, fir, pine, balsam, larch and hemlock. Scientists call them the conifers (cone-bearers) or *gymnosperms*. The other kind includes the poplar and birch, which are called *angiosperms*.

The wood-pulp paper you have prepared into a milky fluid for examination under your microscope is filled with cells called *tracheids*. Their appearance under the microscope is indicated by the drawings (*A*) and (*B*) in *Figure 31*. The two kinds furnished by gymnosperm and angiosperm trees are very characteristic, so that you will have little difficulty in identifying them.

(A) *Gymnosperm cells* (Pine, Fir, Spruce, etc.) are long, often extending clear across and out of the low-power field of your microscope. The ends are fairly sharp. The characteristics identifying features are round or oval markings in regular rows which run *lengthwise* of the cells. The sketch indicates both oval and round marks, which often both occur in a single cell.

(B) *Angiosperm cells* (Poplar and Birch) are smaller and broader, and pointed at both ends. Their characteristic markings are rows of tiny dots, or minute pores, which are arranged in rows running *crosswise* of the cells. These angiosperm cells are seen in the microscope field mixed up with long narrow fibres without any characteristic markings.

(C) *Straw cells*. The pulp from paper made from straw and other grass stems contains long slender fibres knotted at regular intervals. These are frequently pointed at the ends, and have a narrow canal inside, which is constricted at each knot. For straw pulp you will also see cells from the outer skin of the stems and cells from the inner or pith layer of the straw. (See *Figure 31*.)

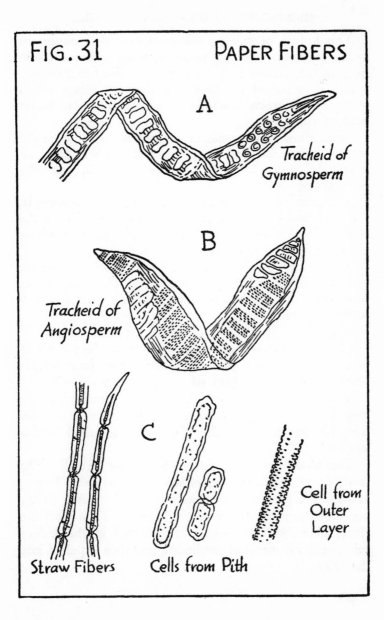

FIG. 31   PAPER FIBERS

A

Tracheid of
Gymnosperm

B

Tracheid of
Angiosperm

C

Straw Fibers   Cells from Pith   Cell from
Outer
Layer

This branch of medical science is extremely important in life insurance and in diagnosing many diseased conditions of the kidneys and other organs. We can give only a hint of some of the most characteristic things which you may see when examining a sample of urine under your microscope.

First allow it to settle in a test-tube until the solid matter is accumulated at the bottom. Then draw off a few drops of this with a pointed glass dipping tube or medicine dropper.

The principal objects which you may see are crystals, red and white blood cells, epithelial cells (from the lining of the kidney) and "tube-casts." These features are identified for your eye at (*A*) in *Figure 32*.

The crystals are *uric acid, acid urates, calcium oxalate* and *ammonium magnesium phosphate. Uric acid* occurs in clusters of rhombic (diamond shape) prisms, which sometimes look like tiny whetstones.

Acid urates are seen in formless, granular masses.

Calcium oxalate occurs in octahedral (eight-sided) crystals. In some positions they show four shapes like the areas on the back of a straight-flap envelope.

Ammonium magnesium phosphate is identified by its long or short prisms with beveled edges, appearing something like square-cut jewels. They are also called "coffin-shaped."

The blood cells are either "white" or "red." The white are much larger. *Epithelial* cells are still larger, and show a prominent central spot or "nucleus." They are shed from the lining of the kidney. *Tube casts* are clear, glass-like rods which are formed in the kidney tubes by some diseased conditions, and then expelled into the urine.

Fig. 32   URINE ANALYSIS

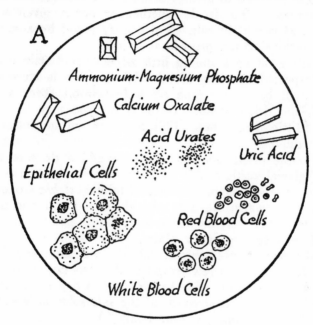

A

Ammonium-Magnesium Phosphate

Calcium Oxalate

Acid Urates

Uric Acid

Epithelial Cells

Red Blood Cells

White Blood Cells

BLOOD TEST CRYSTALS [Haematin]

B

A SIMPLE MICRO-CHEMICAL TEST FOR IDENTIFYING
BLOODSTAINS

Here we are entering the field of the scientific detective who is required to give evidence that a murder has been committed! To decide whether or not a given stain is blood is not difficult. To identify blood by a simple micro-chemical test proceed as follows:

Scrape off on a slide a little of the dried stain which is suspected of being blood. If the stain is on wood, you will have to scrape off a few wood fibres along with the dried blood. If on cloth, you may have to cut a little of the cloth. This, however, will not interfere with the test.

To the dried blood on the slide add a drop or two of "glacial acetic acid." This is obtainable from druggists or photo-supply houses. Holding it high over a gas stove, warm the slide with the blood and acid until the acid is entirely evaporated.

The next step is to place a few drops of a very weak solution of common salt on the slide and heat carefully until entirely evaporated. Do not allow the temperature of the slide to exceed 120 degrees Fahrenheit. The correct strength of the salt solution is seven-hundredths of one per cent (0.07%).

To prepare the salt solution: Dissolve in one ounce of water all the salt it will take up. Allow undissolved salt to settle, and draw off a little of this "saturated" salt solution with a medicine dropper. Place in a test tube. Then add six drops of salt solution to a pint of water (16 ounces). This will be near enough for practical purposes. Place some of this diluted salt solution in a bottle and keep it to make blood tests with.

After the salt solution is entirely evaporated from the slide, place upon it another drop of the glacial acetic acid. This time you must cautiously heat the slide until the drop of acid boils. It will then evaporate very quickly. When dry and cool, examine the slide under the highest power of your microscope, and look for the characteristic crystals of *"haemin"* which indicate the presence of blood. (See (*B*) in *Figure 32.*)

Haemin crystals are minute flat rhomboids (diamond shaped) often lying in the form of a short-armed cross.

This test is very sensitive and delicate. It will show the presence of as little as one-twentieth of a milligram of dried blood! The age of the stain does not matter either. In a famous murder case the stains upon some legal papers were proved by this test to be blood—although over sixty years had elapsed!

This is not, however, a test for *human* blood; it merely proves that a certain stain was made by the blood of an animal. The test for human blood is not microscopic in character, unless the individual cells can be obtained fresh. If the stain has dried, a difficult serum test is required, which is beyond the reach of an amateur. You can, however, become expert in detecting the presence of blood, and this alone might sometime give important legal evidence.

These few pages give only a few hints of the possibilities which anyone can develop with a microscope and some leisure time to devote to microscopic detective work.

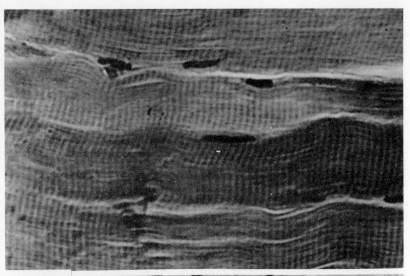

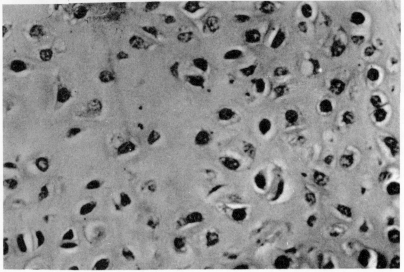

Fig. 33. *Upper photo:* Human voluntary (striated) muscle (magnified 400x).

Courtesy of Herbert A. Fischler

Fig. 34. *Lower photo:* Human cartilage showing cells embedded in cartilage (magnified 385x).

Courtesy of Herbert A. Fischler

VII

LOOKING AT CELLS

About three hundred years ago, Robert Hooke, an English scientist who wrote the first book on microscopic observations, "Micrographia," was looking at a thin slice of cork with a microscope. What he saw resembled the rooms or cells of a monastery. He therefore gave the name "cells" to the little areas that were arranged in order in the cork. Since that time, it has been found that all living things are made of cells.

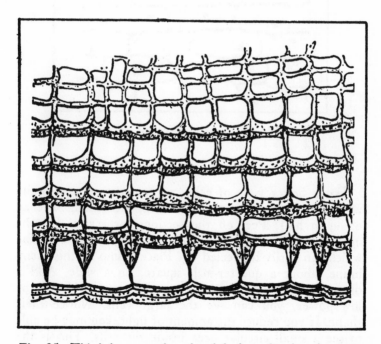

Fig. 35. This is how a section of cork looks under the microscope.

Cut a very thin section of a piece of cork with a sharp razor blade. Place it on a slide, and examine the thinnest part with a microscope. You too will be able to follow in Hooke's footsteps as you see the tiny, evenly-lined up cells.

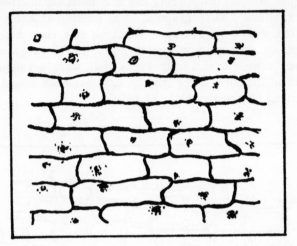

Fig. 36. Onion skin under the microscope.

ONION CELLS

For a better view of cells, we can turn to a common vegetable found in every household, the onion. Slice an onion in half. Peel off the sections, or scales. On the inside of each section you will see a very thin membrane which can easily be peeled off. Place a snip of this membrane, about a quarter-inch square, on a slide. Add a drop of water, and place a cover slip over it. Under the low power, you can see the large cells. Notice their shape. If you reduce the amount of light, you may be able to see a small circular area inside the cells. This is the *nucleus*. Under the high power, it shows more clearly.

There is a way of making the parts of cells more distinct. If a dye or stain is added to the cells, the parts become more outstanding. A common, useful stain is Lugol's iodine. When this is added to the slide, the nucleus becomes sharply defined. You can actually see the structure of the nucleus, including one or more nucleoli inside, under the high power. The cytoplasm, the part of the cell on the outside of the nucleus, also becomes more clearly defined. It is present as very fine granules distributed throughout the inside of the cell.

Both the nucleus and the cytoplasm are living parts of the cell. Together with the cell membrane that covers the outside of the cytoplasm, they make up the protoplasm. Protoplasm is the name given to all the living material of a cell. On the outside, is the non-living cell wall. This supports the cells, and gives them their shape.

You may not be able to see the cell membrane, because it is located right up against the cell wall. However, there is a way of separating it away from the cell wall. Make up a salt solution, by adding a teaspoon of salt to half a glass of water. Add a drop of this to the slide. After a few minutes, you will notice that the protoplasm is shrinking away from the cell wall. Now you will be able to observe the cell membrane on the outside of the cytoplasm. All living things are made of cells, and all cells contain protoplasm. Protoplasm, in turn, consists of a dense part, the nucleus, the liquid part, or the cytoplasm, and the outer part of the cytoplasm, the cell membrane.

THE CELLS OF THE BODY

You can use your microscope to see some of the cells of your own body. No, it is not necessary to use a sharp knife to cut away a portion of your skin, or any other part to make this study. All you need is a toothpick!

You can easily see some of the cells that make up the cheek lining by making a slide in the following way. Gently scrape the inside of your cheek two or three times with the broad end of a toothpick. Then spread the wet material across a clean slide, without applying too much pressure. Since these cells are being transferred away from their natural position, their shape will become distorted if you apply too much pressure when placing them on the slide. Now, add a drop or two of methylene blue or Lugol's iodine stain; ordinary ink that has been filtered may also be used. Carefully place a cover slip over it, and examine with the low power.

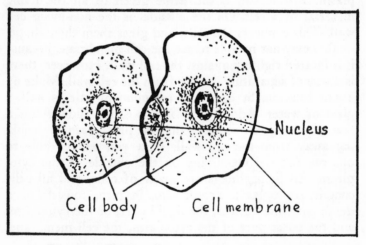

Fig. 37. Cheek cells seen under the microscope.

Under the microscope, you will see small collections of cells. Look for little masses that have been stained by the dye. These cells are quite small. Notice their five-sided shape. Compare several cells in order to make out the general shape. See how the cells are attached to each other. Do you see the nucleus in the center of each? It has a deeper color.

Under the high power, you can see more of the details. The outside of the cell is the cell membrane. The granular material within it, is the cytoplasm. You will probably see the granules that make up the nucleus, too.

MUSCLE CELLS

Another type of cell, is found in the muscles of your arm or leg. Such voluntary muscle tissue can be seen in a small piece of ordinary beef. To make a slide, simply pull apart a tiny piece of beef, about an eighth of an inch in size, with two pins. Be sure to spread the beef apart as well as possible, so that the fibers separate out. Stain with Lugol's iodine, or methylene blue, by adding one or two drops to the material, and cover with a cover slip.

Under the microscope, you can distinguish the individual fibers that make up this type of muscle (See page 94). Notice the stripes, or *striations*, that run across the fibers? This is characteristic of voluntary muscle tissue. These alternating dark and light bands are present in all muscles that can be moved at will.

CARTILAGE

Speaking of beef, if you have a part of the end of a bone, you can also see some of the cells that make up cartilage. They are found in the shiny, smooth part of the end of a bone (See page 94). With a sharp razor, slice away a small portion of this cartilage. The thinner the better. Add a stain to it on a slide, and cover with a cover slip. Under the microscope, select the thinnest portion of the section. You can see the cells scattered amidst the solid material that makes up the cartilage. They almost seem like islands in a sea of hard material. Each cell is in a little space. The cells are generally found in pairs. As the cartilage grows, the cells secrete more of the hard material around themselves.

99

VIII

MICROSCOPIC PETS

THE PARAMECIUM

How would you like to raise a microscopic pet? It may be too small to play with or handle, but it can be watched and studied on the stage of a microscope as it moves rapidly hither and yon. The paramecium is one of the most common of all one-celled animals. You will have little difficulty finding it in any pond water (see *Figure 38*).

To grow paramecium culture at home, this is all you have to do. Obtain a brewer's yeast tablet at a drug store, and crumble it in a glass of water. Then, add some water taken from a pond, containing paramecium, to this glass; a half full medicine-dropper will be enough. Put the glass aside in a shaded spot. In about a week, if you hold the glass up to the light, you will see it swarming with tiny specks that are moving about. These are the paramecia.

Place a drop of the culture on a slide. You will see a mob scene of paramecia, twisting, turning, and darting about. They move so quickly that you will have to keep moving the slide in order to be able to follow them.

You will undoubtedly want to slow them down. One of the best ways of doing this is to take a small piece of lens paper, about a half-inch square, and pull it apart very carefully. Just before the two ends come apart, place it on a slide, and then add your drop of culture at the spot where the two parts have almost separated. Under the microscope, you will see that the paramecia have become trapped. They keep bumping into the fibers of the lens paper. This compels them to stay in a smaller area of the slide, and enables you to get a better look at them.

Now you can see how it appears to glide along. It is propelled by little hair-like projections called cilia, which surround it on all sides. These cilia beat like so many oars, and propel the paramecium in quick darts. It may be easier to see the beating cilia if you reduce the amount of light striking the slide, by adjusting the diaphragm. A higher magnification, of course, also helps.

How does the paramecium eat? You will see how food particles enter, if you add some carmine particles to a small amount of the culture. These particles do not dissolve in the water, but remain suspended as tiny grains. Under the high power, look at the middle part of a paramecium that has stopped moving for a while. You will see a funnel-like section that has beating cilia. This is the mouth. The movement of the cilia creates a current that sweeps in any small materials nearby. As these particles are swept in, you will see them collect at the end of the mouth tube into a small food vacuole. This grows to a certain size, and becomes detached. It then moves around within the protoplasm of the paramecium. You will probably see many of these food vacuoles inside one paramecium. The food is digested there.

You will be interested in seeing the "stinging hairs" or *trichocysts* of a paramecium. Place a drop of ordinary fountain-pen ink on a slide, together with a drop of paramecium culture. Add a cover slip. You will notice that the paramecia have been killed by the ink. However, before they died, they shot out many of these long hairs which you now see on the micro-organism. It is thought by scientists that the paramecium uses these long hairs to protect itself against other tiny animals that may be annoying it. The irritating material or trichocysts keeps them away.

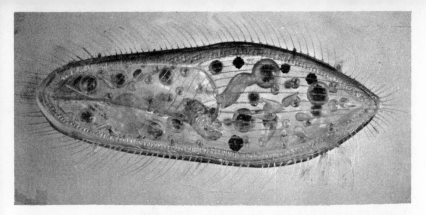

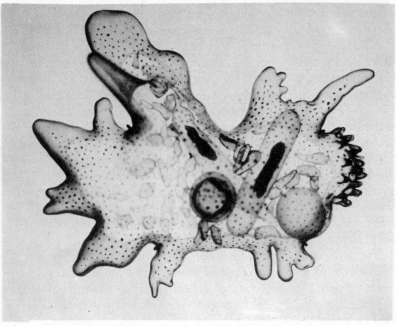

Fig. 38. *Upper photo :* The Paramecium, one of the most common of one-celled animals.

Fig. 39. *Lower photo:* One of the simplest of all living animals, the microscopic, single-celled animal, the Amoeba.

Courtesy of American Museum of Natural History

When a paramecium has grown to its largest possible size, it reproduces. It does this by splitting into two separate parts. Each then swims away, a completely new paramecium. When conditions are right, a paramecium reproduces in this way every hour. You can imagine how many can be formed in a day at this rate. The number runs into the millions. You may often be able to see a paramecium in the process of reproducing when you examine a thick culture.

THE AMOEBA

Amoebae are usually found on the under surface of water lily pads or on the stems of water plants. If you carefully transfer some of the slimy material from there to a slide, and cover it with a cover slip, you may see the grayish, granular jelly-like mass of protoplasm that makes up an amoeba. It moves by "flowing" into its extensions or "pseudopods" (or false feet). It has no particular shape, since it is always flowing in this manner (see *Figure 39*.)

The amoeba may come in contact with some food particle as it moves. It simply flows around and over it, and eats by engulfing the food particle in this way. There is no mouth or other opening through which the food enters. After the food has become part of the amoeba, it is digested by its living protoplasm. Look for small dense portions in the protoplasm that are larger than the tiniest granules; there are the places where the food is being digested.

You may wonder how the amoeba breathes. It takes its oxygen right out of the surrounding water through its cell membrane. This membrane is porous to certain elements such as dissolved oxygen. The amoeba gives off carbon dioxide as a waste material right through this membrane into the surrounding water.

IX

BLOOD — THE LIFE STREAM

The chance are that the only time you have ever seen blood is when you cut your finger, and some of the blood flowed out. How would you like to watch blood flowing around within the blood vessels? Your microscope can reveal this sight to you, just as it first did for Leeuwenhoek, over three hundred years ago.

All you really need is a medium-sized goldfish. First prepare a piece of absorbent cotton about two inches square. Soak it under the faucet so that it is full of water. Remove the goldfish from the water and wrap its head and the front part of its body in the soaked absorbent cotton. If the cotton surrounds these parts of the fish thoroughly, it can be kept alive out of water for as much as twenty minutes.

Now, place the fish on a small glass plate large enough to cover the stage of the microscope. If you have a petri dish, you can use half of it to hold the fish. Now spread out the tail of the fish on the glass. Examine it with the low power of the microscope. If the fish flips its tail out of focus, it would be a good idea to hold the tail in place with half of a microscope slide.

Look for the blood circulating within the small blood vessels. The tiny round structures are the blood cells. Notice how many of them there are. There are millions! In some of the blood vessels, they pass along in single file. These are the smallest blood vessels, the capillaries. As you trace a capillary along, you will see that it connects with another capillary, or else it may join a larger blood vessel, such as a vein or an artery.

Some of the small arteries can be recognized because the blood goes through them in spurts. This is due to the pumping action of the heart. Every time the heart beats, it sends the blood into the arteries which expand under the great pressure, and then relax again to their normal width. This sudden expansion of the artery, each time the heart beats, produces the pulse. The other larger blood vessels through which the blood flows with a steady movement are the veins. As you move the slide around, you can distinguish the three types of blood vessels from each other.

Turn to high power. Now you can see the blood cells a little more clearly. They appear orange-pink in color, and are football-shaped. In the center of each, you can make out the nucleus. These are the red blood cells. When millions of them are gathered into a drop, they make the blood appear red in color. Here and there, you may be able to see other cells being carried along. They are gray in color and may not have any particular shape. These are the white blood cells.

By this time, it may be necessary to return the fish to water. Simply remove the absorbent cotton before you do so. Usually the fish will swim about actively. However, if it floats on its side, you may have to revive it. This can be done by holding the fish's tail, and "dunking" its head in and out of the water about a dozen times. This action causes a fresh supply of water to stream past the gills in a very short time, and helps the fish recover more rapidly.

YOUR OWN BLOOD

If you would like to examine a sample of your own blood, follow this procedure. Swab the tip of your little finger with a piece of absorbent cotton that has been dipped in alcohol. This sterilizes the end of the finger. Pass a needle through a flame once or twice to sterilize it too. After a moment for cooling, prick the soft part of the tip of the finger with the needle. Touch the drop of blood that oozes out to a clean slide. Spread the blood out in a thin film with the edge of the narrow side of another

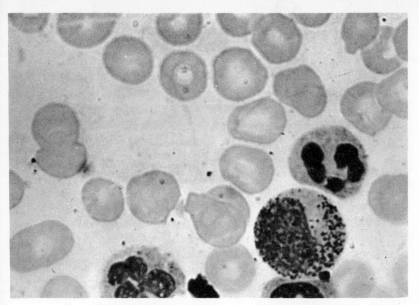

Fig. 40. Human blood cells as seen under oil immersion (magnified 1000x).

Courtesy of Herbert A. Fischler

slide. Allow this smear to dry. Under the high power of the microscope, you will see that the red blood cells are round and pinkish-orange in color. They are shaped like coins (see *Figure 40*). The center part is thinner than the outer edge. There is one unusual feature about human red blood cells; they do not have a nucleus. The blood owes its color to the presence of all these red blood cells. If they were removed from the liquid part of the blood, the plasma, the blood would be straw-colored.

The white blood cells are not as numerous as the red blood cells. They are somewhat larger in size and grayish in color. In most cases they contain a large nucleus. There are several types of white blood cells which an expert can learn to recognize. For anyone interested in studying more about blood cells, there is a special stain called Wright's Stain prepared for this purpose.

X
STARTING THE STUDY OF BACTERIA

You do not need very elaborate equipment to enter the field of bacteriology. A microscope with a high power objective that gives magnifications up to 430 times will be good for many interesting hours spent viewing these tiny organisms.

BACTERIA FROM THE MOUTH

A good place to start is your teeth. Scrape off some of the white material from the molars with a toothpick. Put a drop of water on a slide. Then, spread this material as thinly as you can in this drop of water. When it is dry, "fix" the bacteria by passing the slide quickly through a flame two or three times. This kills the bacteria, and at the same time, glues them to the slide so that they will not wash off when stained.

The slide is then ready to be stained. This is necessary if you are to see the bacteria clearly. Otherwise, they would be colorless, and difficult to observe. The stain dyes them and makes them stand out against a clear background.

A good stain is methylene blue. This can be obtained in a drugstore. Place a drop or two on the part of the slide containing the material from the teeth. Let it remain there for three minutes. Then wash the excess stain off by holding the slide under a gentle flow of water from the faucet.

The slide should be blotted dry between two sheets of filter paper, or allowed to dry in the air. It should *not* be wiped, because wiping will remove the bacteria. A cover slip is not necessary. The slide is now ready to be examined.

Under the high power, you will be able to see the three types of bacteria : the rod-shaped *bacilli;* the round-shaped *cocci;* and the spiral-shaped *spirilla* (see *Fig.* 43–44). These particular bacteria, taken from the teeth, are harmless.

BACTERIA FROM BUTTERMILK

Another good place to find bacteria is in buttermilk. Most of the buttermilk now sold by the large dairies is made by inoculating milk with a type of bacteria called *Streptococcus lactis.* You can buy this buttermilk under the label "cultured." To make a slide of the bacteria, place a drop on a clean slide, and spread it out. After it has dried, place the slide in a small container of alcohol. This removes the fat particles that would otherwise obscure your view of the bacteria. It also fixes the bacteria. After five to ten minutes, stain the slide with methylene blue in the same manner as was done for the teeth bacteria.

When you examine the slide, you will see the chains of round bacteria that are called streptococci. They look like strings of beads. These bacteria are also harmless. As a matter of fact, they are useful to man in that they work for him in the dairy industry to produce buttermilk.

BACTERIA ON PLANT ROOTS

Other useful bacteria are also found growing on the roots of certain plants called legumes, such as beans, clover, and alfalfa. If you carefully dig up one of these plants, so as not to injure the roots, you can wash the soil away gently, and find the little swellings, or nodules on the roots. These nodules contain useful "nitrogen-fixing" bacteria that help provide the plants with important nitrogen compounds that they need for healthy growth.

A slide of these bacteria can be made in this way. Select a small nodule about the size of a pin-head. Crush it between two clean slides that are moved against each other so that the nodule material is smeared over a large part of each slide. Try to spread out the material as much as you can. Then, fix one of the slides in a flame, in the usual way, and stain with methylene blue. When you examine the bacteria under the high power, you will notice their somewhat unusual shape. Most of them will appear rod-shaped. Some, however, seem to have a little bump or projection; others may appear Y-shaped.

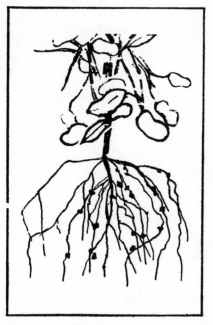

Fig. 41. Bacteria clinging to the roots of a peanut plant.

SAUERKRAUT BACTERIA

Do you like sauerkraut? It is made by the action of another type of useful bacteria on cabbage. You can see living bacteria by looking at a drop of sauerkraut juice.

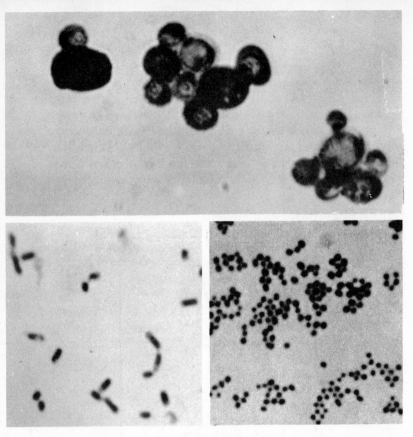

Fig. 42. *Upper photo:* Budding yeast cells (magnified 1000x).

Fig. 43. Bacilli
(magnified 1000x).

Fig. 44. Staphylococci
(magnified 1000x).

Courtesy of Herbert A. Fischler

Place a drop on a clean slide, and cover with a cover
slip. Reduce the amount of light somewhat, so that you
can see the bacteria which will be colorless. You will
see them twisting and turning about. Some move in a
straight line for a short distance and then seem to dis-
appear as they go down a little deeper in the drop just
beyond view. To follow them, turn the fine adjustment
of the microscope downward.

XI

YEAST AND MOLDS

BAKING YEAST

The yeast cake that your mother uses in baking contains thousands of tiny plants, each so small that you would need a microscope to see it. To study some yeast cells, crumble a small piece of a yeast cake into a glass of water; add a teaspoon of sugar to it. The sugar is used as food by the yeast plants. As they use up the sugar, they give off a gas called carbon dioxide which you can see bubbling upward in the solution, after a few hours. The yeast plants grow especially rapidly if you put the jar in a warm place.

The following day, put a drop of the solution on a slide. Add a drop of water to this liquid, and put a cover slip over it. There are so many yeast plants on the slide, that unless you dilute them with this drop of water, they will be too close together for you to be able to make out their structure.

Under the low power, all you can see will be tiny cells, so small that they appear to be mere dots. Each of these is a yeast plant or cell. When you turn to the high power, you can see a little more detail about the structure (see *Figure 42*). If you look carefully, you can see a clear area in each cell. This is a vacuole, and is usually filled with food material that is stored by the cell. Attached to many of the yeast cells, you will see tiny projections or buds. As a yeast cell grows, it begins to divide, and pinch off a little part of itself to form a new cell. This method of reproduction is called budding. Sometimes, there may be many buds attached to a larger mother cell.

Yeast is useful in the baking industry because it gives off carbon dioxide, and makes dough rise. Without this action, the bread we eat would be hard-packed and too solid. It would lack the fluffiness caused by the presence of many air spaces. Yeast is also used in the brewing industry because of the action of yeast on sugar to produce alcohol. These two products, carbon dioxide and alcohol are formed by yeast during the fermentation of sugar.

BREAD MOLD

Another interesting small plant is the mold that grows on bread or other food. Most people do not suspect that this mold is a plant that has an interesting history of development. You can study this in the following way: Put a piece of moist blotter in the bottom of a jar. Add a small piece of bread. Now sprinkle some ordinary household dust onto the bread. Seal the jar tightly so that none of the moisture can evaporate. Observe the jar every day for a period of a week and a half.

At first, there seems to be nothing happening. Then, on the second or third day, you will suddenly see some cottony material on the bread. The next day, there will be more of it. This fuzzy, white material will seem to be spreading. A few days later, little black dots will be visible, scattered throughout the fuzz. You will now be able to recognize the mold that has developed on the bread.

To see what this mold looks like under the microscope, prepare a slide by taking a small amount of the mold off the bread or the side of the jar with a pair of forceps. Do not take too much of this material; the slide would become too crowded to reveal anything. Add a drop of water, and cover with a cover slip.

Now the plant can be seen to possess a large ball-like structure at one end. It contains many tiny little cells called spores. In making the slide, you may have broken one of these spore cases, and the spores may be all over the slide. These spores are so small that they cannot be seen without the aid of a microscope. Move the slide and trace the long stem-like structure to which the spore case is attached, until you come to the bottom. Here, you can see the root-like structure which anchors the mold to the bread. From these roots, the food is absorbed into the mold, enabling it to grow (see *Figure 45*).

You may wonder how the mold appeared on the bread in the first place. The dust that you sprinkled on the bread undoubtedly contained many spores. These spores are present everywhere, in dust, in the air, and in the soil. When they have the right conditions of moisture and food, they will germinate and form the mold plant.

THE PENICILLIN MOLD

The ordinary bread mold that we have been discussing is black. Sometimes, a blue-green mold appears on bread, or fruit that has been left in a moist place. This blue-green mold has become quite famous in recent years, because it gives off the substance known as penicillin. The mold itself is called *Penicillium notatum*. It is very common, and was used commercially for many years in making the so-called blue-green cheese, or Rocquefort cheese, before it became famous in medicine. This mold gives the cheese its particular flavor and color.

Under the microscope, *Penicillium* looks a little different from bread mold. Instead of the spores being formed in a round spore case, they appear at the ends of branches, like grapes in a row. These spores, too, are present practically everywhere. When the record stratosphere flight was made in a balloon a number of years ago, it was found that mold spores were present in the atmosphere twelve miles up. They were unaffected by the intense cold because of their heavy protective wall. When these spores were brought down and placed in an incubator, they germinated into mold plants (see *Figure 46*).

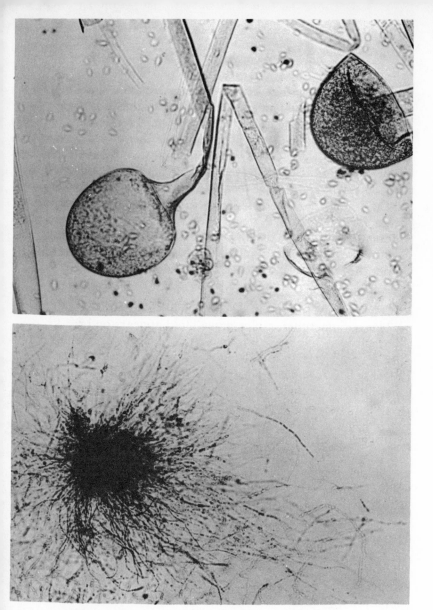

Fig. 45. *Upper photo:* Bread Mold (magnified 100x).
Fig. 46. *Lower photo:* Penicillium Mold (magnified 87x).

Courtesy of Herbert A. Fischler

XII

YOUR MICRO-GARDEN AND ZOO
(PREPARING CULTURES)

As you become better acquainted with the strange world revealed by your microscope, you will want to keep a collection of the microscopic animals and plants for future study. The continuous changes in the lives of the captives in your zoo, their rapid multiplication, their struggles for existence, and their surprising activities will furnish many absorbing hours of instruction and entertainment for you and your friends. To establish a zoo, all you need will be a few simple jars and materials for handling the animals that you will collect and raise.

You have already learned how to collect microscopic big game from the ponds and streams (see pages 48-74). When you return home, remove the lids from your collecting jars (see Fig. 47). Place the jars on a window sill, but protect them from direct sunlight. Some animals can be found in the jars almost immediately. Others will make their appearance in 24 to 48 hours. Most of them will gather at the top of each jar, where they can be collected easily with a medicine dropper. Different kinds of microscopic animals will be found an inch or two beneath the surface, and still others, such as Amoeba, will cling to the bottom of the jar. Explore all these areas with your microscope to find inhabitants for your zoo. Take samplings from different areas, put them on separate well-slides, and try to identify them under your microscope.

You should keep your jars for a number of weeks. As you examine them each day, you will find that the population will change. Some types of animals will die out. Others will appear and multiply. In this way, you will have a steady supply of new animals for your microscopic zoo.

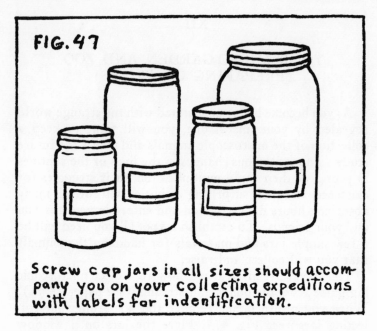

Screw cap jars in all sizes should accompany you on your collecting expeditions with labels for indentification.

HOW TO TRANSFER ANIMALS TO NEW HOMES

When a particular type of animal appears to be at the height of its numbers in a jar, it becomes necessary to transfer it to a new container. This is usually done in such a way, that only that particular type of animal is to be present in the new jar. This is easier if you have medicine droppers with fine-pointed tips. The soft glass of a medicine dropper can be melted quite easily over a gas flame. Heat the middle of the dropper until it is soft (see Fig. 48). Then remove it from the flame. Holding each end in the tips of your fingers, quickly pull in opposite directions until the glass is drawn out to a fine tube (See Fig. 49). Now simply break it at any desired point and you have a fine collecting tube. This can easily pick up a single animal as you watch it under the microscope. If that one

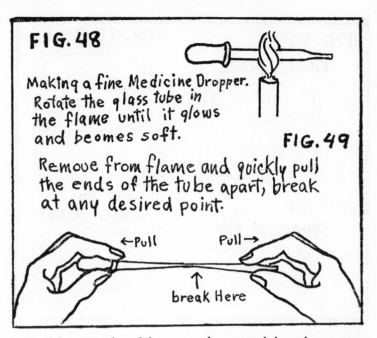

FIG. 48

Making a fine Medicine Dropper. Rotate the glass tube in the flame until it glows and beomes soft.

FIG. 49

Remove from flame and quickly pull the ends of the tube apart, break at any desired point.

←Pull   Pull→

↑
break Here

animal is now placed in a new jar containing the proper food material, it will quickly multiply and soon you will have many thousands, all of the same kind. Instead of using jars, you may wish to purchase special culture dishes from your biological supply store. There are two kinds of dishes. The *finger bowl* (see Fig. 50) is a large container which holds a full cup (8 ounces) of liquid. The *Syracuse dish* (see Fig. 51) is smaller. It holds only a teaspoonful or two, but it can be placed directly on your microscope stage for direct examination (see Fig. 53). Both types can be stacked one on the other for convenient storage (see Fig. 52).

GROWING AMOEBA AND ITS RELATIVES

The amoeba and his cousins have been described on pages 60 and 102. Now let's try growing them.

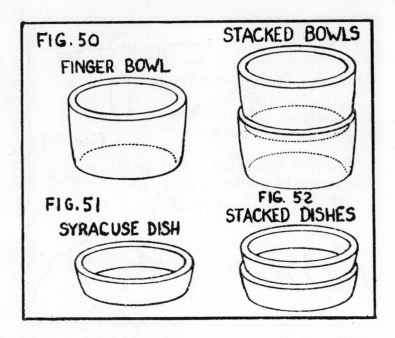

FIG. 50
FINGER BOWL

STACKED BOWLS

FIG. 51
SYRACUSE DISH

FIG. 52
STACKED DISHES

To grow amoeba and its relatives you need pure water and a certain amount of food material. The quality of the water is important, since these tiny animals are easily poisoned by impurities such as lead from water pipes. It is best to collect water from the ponds in which such animals live, and to filter the water through absorbent cotton before use. Aquarium water from any fish tank may also be used. The amoeba and its relatives are not very particular about what they eat, but it is quite important not to overfeed them. If you do, many bacteria will develop, the water will become foul, and your amoeba and its relatives will die. Some of the relatives need more food than others, so here is a chance for you to experiment with different kinds and quantities of foods. You may make an important discovery. Who knows?

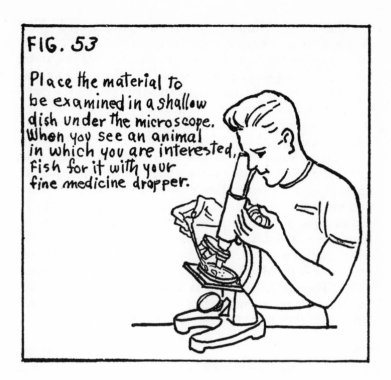

FIG. 53

Place the material to be examined in a shallow dish under the microscope. When you see an animal in which you are interested, fish for it with your fine medicine dropper.

One way to grow amoeba is to boil two one-inch pieces of hay (obtainable from local riding stables) in a half ounce of water and to let this food mixture stand for two days. Then add the amoeba with your fine medicine dropper. Rotifers and many other kinds of animals will also grow in this mixture. From time to time add a dropper full of water. Do not permit the water to become more than one inch deep in the container and keep it loosely covered. As the amoeba and his relatives become very abundant, stir the liquid and pour half of it into another bowl prepared in the same way. This will probably have to be done every six weeks or so.

Other kinds of food materials may also be used. You may use four wheat grains (available at health food stores) instead of hay. Rice grains or small bits of lettuce leaves are good sources of food too. If you wish to grow paramecium, described on pages 100-102, you must supply more food. Use 6 or 8 wheat grains or 10 pieces of hay. A very good growth of paramecium and many other small animals is obtained by boiling two ounces of lettuce leaves in a pint of water until half of the liquid has evaporated. Let this stand for a day or two until the water begins to appear cloudy. Then add your animals. From time to time, add more lettuce water as the jar containing the animals shows signs of losing its cloudiness; but never add more than one teaspoonful at a time. You may also experiment with such food sources as flour, cereal, split peas, or malted milk powder. All of these have been used successfully. The secret is to use as little food as possible and to transfer your animals when you see through the microscope that they have become too crowded.

GROWING WATER FLEAS AND HYDRA

When you find Hydras (see page 64), place them in an aquarium which has no fish in it, or use a large glass jar. They are fed regularly with water fleas, especially Daphnia (see page 70). This is just as entertaining to watch as feeding time in the monkey house at the zoo. Pick up the Daphnia with a medicine dropper and place it close to the Hydra. It will soon be captured by the Hydra's tentacles and devoured. Daphnia can be bought in tropical fish stores, but it is more fun to grow it as part of your zoo. This can be done by making a paste with hard boiled egg yolk and water. Add the paste to a gallon jar of water until it becomes slightly cloudy. Add the egg yolk paste each week as the water clears.

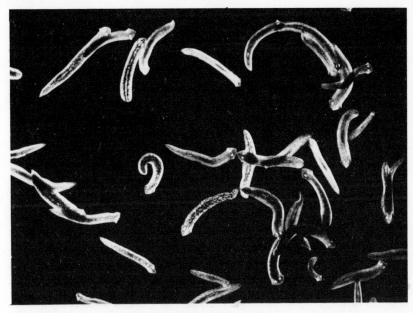

Fig. 54. PLANARIA WORMS IN THE ZOO
Courtesy of Carolina Biological Supply Co., Burlington N.C.

The Planaria (see Fig. 54) is a little flat brown worm,
less than half an inch long. It may be found under stones
in ponds, or on the bottoms of water lily pads, or leaves
of other water plants. It may also be collected by tying
pieces of raw meat to strings and letting them lie in the
water. Place the worms in a white dish in about an inch
of water. Every week, feed them with a very small piece
of fresh liver. The worms will attach themselves to the
meat and should be removed after an hour. Remove the
meat after feeding. Change the water each day, adding
fresh pond water.

There are several very interesting and instructive experiments that anyone can perform successfully with Planaria worms. Can you get worms with two heads or two

tails? Try the following experiments by making different types of cuts (see Fig. 55) and see what happens:

Experiment 1. To grow a worm with two tails, simply make a cut lengthwise with a sharp razor blade as shown by dotted line in Diagram 1.

Experiment 2. If you want a worm with two heads, first cut off the worm's head as shown in Diagram 2; then, make a short lengthwise cut as shown in the same diagram.

Experiment 3. Cut a Planaria worm into 8 pieces, as shown in Diagram 3. Place each piece in a separate Syracuse dish of water and label the dish so that you can tell which section of the body each piece came from. It is not always possible to predict the results of this experiment, but it will produce some strange and interesting creatures.

Experiment 4. Make two diagonal cuts as shown in Diagram 4. The center section will grow a head that will come out at an angle, and a tail that will also grow out at an angle.

Experiment 5. Remove the head at cut 1, and then cut out a triangular piece as shown in cut 2. A normal head will develop at cut 1, and a smaller head at cut 2.

In all cases, after you have made your cuts, place the worms in a dish of clean water. Sometimes the edges of the cuts may start to grow together again. If they do, simply repeat the cuts you made the first time. The process of regrowth may be slow, but be patient. Do not make the mistake of thinking the worms are dead if they do not move after their operation. Continue taking care of them until you have your unusual new specimens. Undoubtedly, you will want to keep a record of these experiments, and you might make sketches of the results.

Use the lowest power on your microscope or a pocket lens when you perform these experiments, and when you view the Planaria in the process of regrowth.

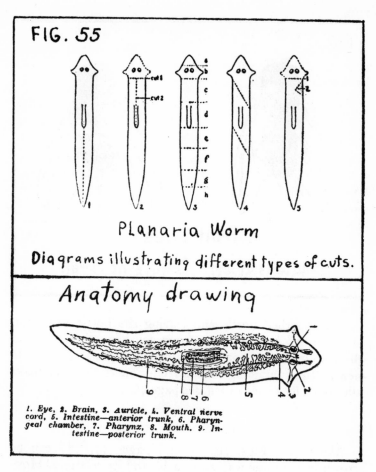

FIG. 55

Planaria Worm

Diagrams illustrating different types of cuts.

Anatomy drawing

1. Eye, 2. Brain, 3. Auricle, 4. Ventral nerve cord, 5. Intestine—anterior trunk, 6. Pharyngeal chamber, 7. Pharynx, 8. Mouth. 9. Intestine—posterior trunk.

THE FAMOUS FRUIT FLY

The little fruit fly (see Fig. 56) has become a well-known character because it has been used to study the laws of heredity. You will find it a fine addition to your zoo because you can use it to study such insect parts as the wings, the compound eyes, and the legs. The flies are easily captured by placing very ripe pieces of banana in

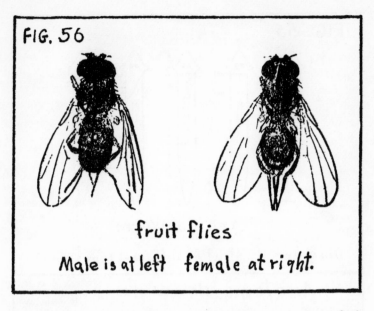

FIG. 56

fruit flies

Male is at left   female at right.

a wide-mouthed bottle and leaving the bottle in a fruit store for an hour or two. After you have obtained your flies, stopper the bottle with cotton. Transfer them to new bottles containing banana from time to time. To make slides of a fly's wing or leg, see page 46.

A GARDEN OF ALGAE

Algae (see Figs. 16, 18 and pages 57, 58) can be grown in the same way as amoeba and its relatives. However, they are very sensitive to poisons and cannot be grown in metal containers. Try making a food supply by boiling a teaspoonful of soil in a quart of pond water or aquarium water. Such algae as desmids and diatoms (see pages 58-60) will grow in this liquid. Some cultures of algae grow slowly and should be kept sealed. Since they are green plants, they need a good supply of light.

Making a garden of bacteria can be done with the few materials you have at home. The basic food is a kind of meat soup. Take one bouillon cube (available at all food stores) and dissolve it in a pint of water. This soup should be placed in small sterilized bottles and sealed with cotton. Sterilization is done by heating the bottles in a pressure cooker at 15 pounds pressure for twenty minutes. Place the bacteria you wish to grow (from your mouth, from buttermilk, or from other sources) in a bottle of the soup. This must be done with a needle which has been heated by passing it through a flame. A suitable needle can be made from nichrome wire, which you can get in a hardware store. Keep the soup in a warm dark place and the bacteria will multiply rapidly. Although a 1000x microscope is preferred for viewing such small objects as bacteria, a 500x is also adequate. If the bacteria are large enough, there's a possibility of seeing them through a 300x microscope.

The biological and laboratory supplies mentioned in this book are obtainable from laboratory supply houses, model and hobby shops, or science departments of department stores near you. If you have difficulty obtaining them from local sources, you might write for a catalogue to any of the following, which represent a small part of the many science supply houses around the country:

Atlas Scientific Co., 14309 Ilene, Detroit 38, Mich.

Cambosco Scientific Co., 37 Antwerp St., Brighton Station, Boston 35, Mass.

Carolina Biological Supply Co., Burlington, North Carolina

Coe-Palm Co., 1130 N. Milwaukee Avenue, Chicago 22, Ill.

Consolab Corp., 5 Park East Drive, Garden City, New York

Clinton Misco Co., 6780 Jackson Road, Ann Arbor, Mich.

Dennoyer-Geppert Co., 52-35 N. Ravenswood Ave., Chicago 40, Ill.

Edmunds Scientific Corp., Barrington, New Jersey

Frey Scientific Co., 271-273 Orange Street, Mansfield, Ohio

J. E. Griffin Co., 216 East 11th Street, Kansas City, Mo.

Laabs Company, 1937 West Vliet Street, Milwaukee, Wisc.

Micro Service Co., 803 Providence Road, Media, Pa.

National Biological Laboratories, P.O. Box 511, Vienna, Va.

National Biological Supplies, 2325 S. Michigan Ave., Chicago 16, Ill.

Perfect Parts, One North Haven Street, Baltimore 24, Md.

Physio Chem Corp., 208 S. 14th Avenue, Mt. Vernon, New York

Porter Chemical Co., Hagerstown, Md.

Rueters Scientific Co., 3034 N. Francisco St., Chicago 18, Ill.

Stansi Corp., 1231 N. Honore Street, Chicago 22, Ill.

Sherwin Scientific Co., North 1112 Ruby St., Spokane 2, Wash.

Scientific Supplies Co., 600 S. Spokane Street, Seattle 4, Wash.

Ward's Natural Science Estab. 300 Ridge Road, E. Rochester 3, N. Y.

Williams Brown & Earle, 904 Chestnut Street, Phila. 7, Pa.

Western Scientific Co., 5348 Auburn Blvd., Sacramento 21, Calif.